Recognising and Sup
Able Children
in Primary Schools

Hilary Lee-Corbin
and Pam Denicolo

David Fulton Publishers
London

David Fulton Publishers
2 Park Square, Milton Park, Abingdon, Oxon OX14 4RN

270 Madison Avenue, New York, NY 10016

First published in Great Britain in 1998 by David Fulton Publishers
Transferred to digital printing

David Fulton Publishers is an imprint of the Taylor & Francis Group, an informa business

British Library Cataloguing in Publication Data
A catalogue record for this book is available from the British Library.

ISBN 1-85346-555-0

Typeset by Helen Skelton, London

Contents

Preface

The purpose of this book is to raise awareness among teachers and parents about the factors which influence under-achievement in able children in the primary years. In the past there has been a dearth of research focused on able children of this age, especially in the UK. In order to fill this perceived deficit, this book is based on a research project which incorporated interviews and observation in context, as well as traditional testing procedures. In this study, therefore, the views of parents, teachers and children were considered and all were given voice to provide a holistic picture of the situation.

The importance of opportunity and motivation is emphasised in addition to recognition of innate ability if an able child is to succeed and realise potential. The significance of a partnership between parents and teachers in the education of able children is highlighted.

Able children have not always been thought of as requiring an education particularly tailored to suit their needs, since it has been assumed by many that their ability meant that they would succeed regardless of other factors. The authors suggest that this argument is flawed and present a number of case studies which exemplify this proposal.

It is acknowledged that contemporary teachers lead busy and pressurised professional lives, but it is suggested that untold benefits can arise if they take the time to get to know their pupils and investigate their perspectives, especially those which constrain and enhance their achievement. Ways in which this can be effected by the class teacher through personal construct psychology techniques are proposed alongside suggestions for improving the collaboration between parents and teachers.

Acknowledgements

We wish to express our thanks to all those teachers, parents and children who participated in this study. We sincerely hope that the insights provided by this research will be of use to them.

We also wish to thank Mr Mark Verity and Mrs Jan Cope who read and gave their opinions on the text. Particular thanks go to Dr Malcolm Corbin for his support and advice.

Every effort was made to trace John T. Wood, author of 'Poem for Everyman', published in *How do you Feel?* This poem is reproduced on page 143 and the publishers will be pleased to hear from readers who can locate Mr Wood so as to make amends in future editions.

Chapter 1

Introduction and Background

Able children are an asset to a school, as any teacher will tell you, and for the majority of the time, a joy to teach because they quickly absorb and assimilate new information. However, they can present difficulties for both parents and teachers as they are often not the easiest of people to live with and can present problems at school. Keeping their motivation alive and constantly presenting them with challenge can be a headache for a teacher in a busy mixed-ability classroom. At times though, because a teacher in a primary school is under so much pressure trying to cater for the needs of all in his/her care, able children do not always receive the time and attention they deserve. In addition, the under-achieving able child is often overlooked because his/her performance may be on a par with the average child. They are not easy to detect and it is incumbent on the teacher to be vigilant to any signs which may reveal ability and then to investigate further.

This book sets out to help teachers and parents to identify factors characteristic of achieving and under-achieving able children and tentatively offers suggestions about how they might cope with able children and their associated problems.

First, this chapter looks at various definitions of ability which are to be found in the literature on able children, and then follows this with a discussion of the opinions which the teachers involved in Lee-Corbin's research had about able children. It continues with an overview of the book, setting out the main points covered in each of the chapters.

Definitions of the able child

There is no generally accepted definition of what constitutes an able or gifted child, nor are the labels used consistently. The HMI report on the education of very able children in maintained schools cited a number of definitions, including children who demonstrate: a high general intellectual ability; a specific aptitude in one or more subjects; creative or productive thinking; leadership qualities; ability in creative or performing arts and psychomotor ability (HMI, 1992).

Galton (1869) used the term *genius* to denote people of very superior ability.

Terman used the term *gifted* for children of high intelligence and it is possibly his influence which made this term so popular (Terman and Oden, 1926). For Terman, children who scored 140 or above on a scale of intelligence were thought of as being gifted. There seems to be a considerable difference of opinion about where on the Intelligence Quotient (IQ) scale the cut off point for ability/giftedness should be. For Terman, it was the top 2 per cent whereas others such as DeHaan and Havighurst (1957) thought that children in the top 10 per cent of the ability spectrum should be thought of as gifted. There have been others however, who have thought of giftedness as any highly accomplished mature performance (Witty, 1951). It follows from these comments that ability has not always been seen solely in terms of an IQ score and indeed the debate continues.

Talent was also a term used in connection with ability. In some cases, *talented* or *academically talented* came to be used as a lower level of giftedness, with the latter reserved for those of particular intellectual ability (Feldhusen and Jarwan, 1993). Other people used the term *talent* to denote an ability in non-academic fields, for example in dance, music or sport.

Gardner and Clark (1992) looked on ability as being multi-dimensional. They saw intelligence as a complex of aptitudes or intelligences, learned skills and knowledge, motivations, interests, attitudes and dispositions which make it possible for an individual to succeed in an occupation or vocation.

Renzulli's definition may also be viewed as multi-dimensional, consisting of above average general ability, high levels of task commitment and high levels of creativity (Renzulli, 1986). Within Renzulli's theory, for an able person to achieve there must be present non-intellectual traits such as the capacity and willingness to work hard.

Tannenbaum's model (1983) encompassed both potential and achievement. Not only must children have general ability and certain personality attributes to succeed, but they must also live in the sort of environment which would foster that talent.

Gagné (1991), on the other hand, saw ability in terms of potential. Talent was viewed as the end product, providing that potential for the development of this talent existed in the first place. Potential could only be translated into various talents if certain catalysts were present, for example parental or teacher support.

This synopsis of viewpoints from the literature indicates that there is some debate about whether ability is a general predisposition or has a specific focus. Certainly it is clear that it is not always identifiable; potential may exist but be unrealised in a specific context.

For the puposes of this book, the term *able* will be used to denote children of high ability and for the purposes of Lee-Corbin's research which is described in this book, able children were seen as the top 10 per cent of the ability spectrum.

The teachers who participated in this study had their own opinions as to what constituted an able child. It was felt that these views were important as they represented attitudes and values which could possibly affect the children under consideration. Consequently, this chapter explores teachers' ideas and definitions of high ability. It incorporates the opinions of teachers who felt that ability was general and the opinions of teachers who thought that ability was more specific.

Teachers' views of an able child who is a *good all-rounder*

For four of the twelve teachers who participated in this study, high ability meant a child showing this ability generally and being a *good all-rounder*. The following comment came from a teacher who felt that, to be considered highly able, a child must be capable of producing work required by the task. However, this does not allow for a highly able child who has a learning difficulty or has concentration problems:

> An able child is one that understands immediately and can produce the work necessary. An able child is usually good at everything – an all-rounder.

Skills of listening and concentration were also felt to be necessary if a child was to achieve:

> [An able child is] a child who has the ability to reach their potential. They should have the skills of listening and concentrating.

Another concept introduced by one teacher was that of the able child knowing exactly what response was required and being able to meet that expectation:

> Someone who performs well in all curriculum areas and is capable of achieving. Someone who is attuned to the system and copes.

In addition to this, four teachers emphasised an able child's ability to think broadly and to seek out information:

> Generally they're good across the board. They are receptive to information. They should be capable of thinking around a subject and of going and finding further information.

Only one teacher in this group felt that such children met with failures in some respect. He was of the opinion that highly able children were not good on the sports field:

> An able child is one who has an all-round command of many subjects. In my experience, children who are able in academic subjects are not able on the sporting side.

This may be so in this teacher's experience, but the idea of the able child as puny and bespectacled, whose only interest is books, has long been refuted (Terman and Oden, 1926).

Figure 1.1 summarises these comments.

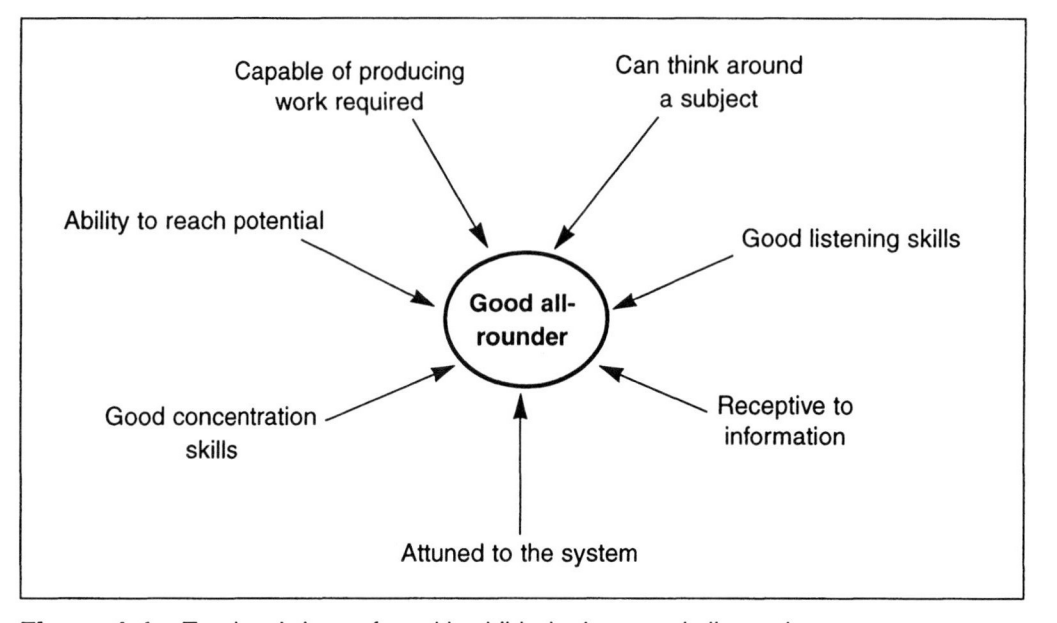

Figure 1.1   Teachers' views of an able child who is a *good all-rounder*

All the teachers quoted above felt that able children were 'generally good at most things'. Others, however, felt that high ability was more specific.

Teachers' views of an able child who had specific skills

Six of the twelve teachers were of the opinion that ability was specific. In the following comment, the teacher saw specific ability as emerging at the upper end of the junior school:

> Ability seems to be specific and not across the board. At certain younger stages, it appears across the board. It's when knowledge has been learnt that ability breaks down more into areas.

Three teachers in this group linked ability with thinking creatively, associating this with lateral or divergent thinking. One teacher thought of an able child as being:

> A child who excels, thinks in an unusual, strange, creative way.

This is connected with the next comment, with its emphasis on the ability to express thoughts and ideas:

> … a child who shows a special aptitude towards anything, academic, sporting – any area of the curriculum. A child who is able to express opinions and ideas and assimilates new ideas quickly.

The ability to ask questions for which there may not be definite answers, to think for themselves, was seen by one teacher to be a mark of ability:

> An able child is one who understands and extends. It's the child who wants to outstrip the rest of the class. They really want to take things a stage further. It's the ability to ask 'what if'.

While many would agree with this comment in essence, not every able child is necessarily competitive. Indeed, competitiveness may be socially developed. Both parents and the school can influence a child's attitude towards competition. It may be emphasised or discouraged, depending on the ethos of the school or the outlook of the parent.

An idea which occurred on a number of occasions during the interviews was that an able child was one who was capable of playing with concepts:

> An able child is one who, if you give it a concept, grasps it very quickly and can throw it around in their mind to good effect.

Perhaps associated with this willingness to think about new ideas is the concept of motivation. Motivation was perceived by all of the teachers in this section as being linked with ability:

> An able child finds no difficulty with work, is able to go deeply into a subject, has inner resources and is interested enough to find things out for himself [*sic*].

This definition, though, does not allow for the able under-achiever, whose abilities have yet to be developed, or indeed an able child who has a specific learning difficulty.

The picture which has emerged so far is one of an able child who is successful and confident. The teacher who made the following comment associated personality traits with ability:

> An able child is one who is inquisitive, a perfectionist, highly self-critical, bubbly, alive. In my opinion, you rarely get an able child who is withdrawn. An able child appears different in every way. Also he/she has strong opinions about things.

Connecting ability and personality is perhaps unwise, as it gives rise to the sort of myths which researchers have been at pains to dispel for a number of years (Terman and Oden, 1926; Gross, 1993). The able child who is shy and retiring is not uncommon.

Figure 1.2 summarises these opinions. Thus there were some teachers who felt that ability was general; others felt that it was specific. Typically, they did not think that it could be either one or the other. Only two teachers thought of ability in that way, as exemplified in the following comment:

> A child can be able in one or in many directions. He/she is not necessarily able in all academic curriculum areas.

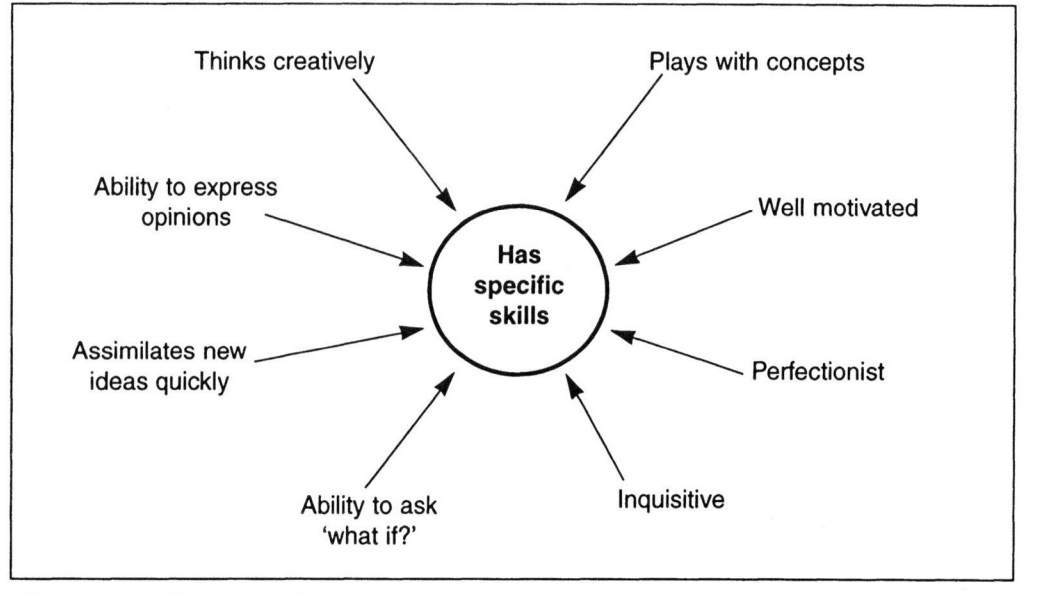

Figure 1.2   Teachers' views of the able child who has ability in specific skills

It was this divergence of opinion that we met in our professional work with teachers, and the wide range of children who stretched our own abilities as teachers, that led to further exploration of the issues associated with achieving and under-achieving children in the local context. This book summarises the results of the study.

Overview

Chapter 2 discusses key theories and studies which have influenced international thought on able children in recent years. Research on ability in general and on under-achievement is discussed and evaluated.

A review of current educational provision for the able is to be found in Chapter 3 and encompasses surveys conducted by the National Association for Gifted Children (NAGC) and HMI. This chapter concludes with a discussion of curriculum strategies commonly used in the education of the able.

In Chapter 4 the research strategy adopted for the Lee-Corbin study is set out, detailing both the quantitative and qualitative aspects. It explores the fundamental reasoning on which the research was based and the different ways in which the data was collected.

The results of the study are to be found in Chapter 5 and include models of the typical achieving and under-achieving able child and factors associated with their performance.

Chapters 6 and 7 contain vignettes or case studies of achieving and under-achieving able children. These were drawn from data collected from interviews, observation and children's narratives, drawing together a range of perspectives.

Chapter 8 looks at what has been learnt from the research and how this can help schools to improve their provision for able children, exploring in the conclusion ways in which a policy for the able child can be drawn up.

In Chapter 9, personal construct psychology methods are introduced as ways in which teachers can get to know their children better so that they can understand and help them.

Advice to parents is to be found in Chapter 10 and draws on the experiences of the parents who participated in the Lee-Corbin study. In many cases this advice has been tried and tested by parents who have able children of their own.

Chapter 11 attempts to draw together threads discussed earlier and gives the last words to the participants.

This chapter began with a review of definitions of able children and the next chapter takes this one step further by considering current theories and research to which these definitions may be linked.

Chapter 2

Key Research on Able Children

When considering the education of able children questions are raised about the nature of human abilities, society's values, under-achievement and related influences. This chapter sets the scene for our discussion of able children in that it presents relevant research which has been carried out in these areas both in Britain and in other parts of the world. The first section in this chapter looks at recent theories of intelligence to give context to the discussion of the results of particular research projects which follow.

Theories of intelligence

In the past, intelligence was thought of as a unitary entity which could be measured for an individual to provide a score demonstrating 'general intelligence' as compared with the rest of the population. Modern theories of intelligence recognise that 'intelligence' is a complex notion. For instance, Gardner suggested that individuals differ in their cognitive development because there are different and partially independent sorts of intelligence that are domain specific (1983). In his theory of multiple intelligences he put forward the idea that there exist: 'several relatively autonomous human intellectual competencies', or what he describes as 'multiple intelligences' (Gardner, 1983, p. 8).

These are relatively independent of each other and can be combined in a number of different ways. They are:

1. linguistic intelligence;
2. musical intelligence;
3. logico-mathematical intelligence;
4. spatial intelligence;
5. bodily-kinaesthetic intelligence (dancing, acting);
6. personal intelligence or knowledge of self and others. (Gardner, 1983, p. 8).

In proposing that cognitive development is domain specific, Gardner provided an explanation for the child who has particular abilities in a specific area.

Intelligence has also been seen to be multi-faceted by a number of other theorists, including Renzulli.

Intelligence to Renzulli comprised a very wide array of cognitive and other skills. He thought that to be an exceptional performer takes much more than brain power. Within his theory, without the support of non-intellectual traits such as the capacity and willingness to work hard to achieve excellence, it was impossible to achieve highly. He defined giftedness as consisting of three factors representing above-average ability, task commitment and creativity (see Figure 2.1). He felt that all three factors should be present before a child could be considered to be gifted.

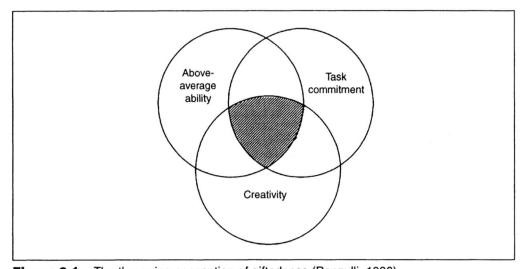

Figure 2.1   The three-ring conception of giftedness (Renzulli, 1986)

The importance of this model was that it recognised that non-intellectual traits such as task commitment were important for achievement, but it does not allow us to identify and help the under-achieving able child whose motivation and task commitment are low.

In the light of this theory, it appears essential for teachers to find ways of motivating able children to avoid loss of potential. Another theory, that of Tannenbaum, also incorporates task commitment, together with necessary environmental factors that support the development and realisation of potential.

As can be seen from Tannenbaum's model, Figure 2.2 (Tannenbaum, 1983), giftedness encompassed both potential and achievement which are dependent on the presence of several factors. Not only must children have general ability and certain personality attributes to succeed, but they must also live in the sort of environment which would foster that talent. Tannenbaum cited five factors which in active combination made for excellence:

1. *General ability*: This is the testable ability, using traditional indices such as IQ tests.

2. *Special ability*: In addition to being able to think well, a gifted person must have special abilities for some particular area if he/ she is to be recognised as gifted.
3. *Non-intellectual factors*: A child will not succeed unless his/her ability was accompanied by other factors such as motivation, secure self-esteem and the capacity to stay on task.
4. *Environmental factors*: Tannenbaum stressed the importance of a child's family and school in the development of high ability. However, he also felt that the amount of investment that society was prepared to make to ensure success was crucial. It appeared that this was a point which had not been specifically addressed by other researchers, although cultural influences had been noted.
5. *Chance factors*: The influence that these may have on an individual must not be under-estimated. A chance meeting with just the right person to advance one's career or studies can make the difference between succeeding or not. Again, this was not a topic often discussed by researchers.

Tannenbaum argued that when these factors combined, they produced a mesh of excellence.

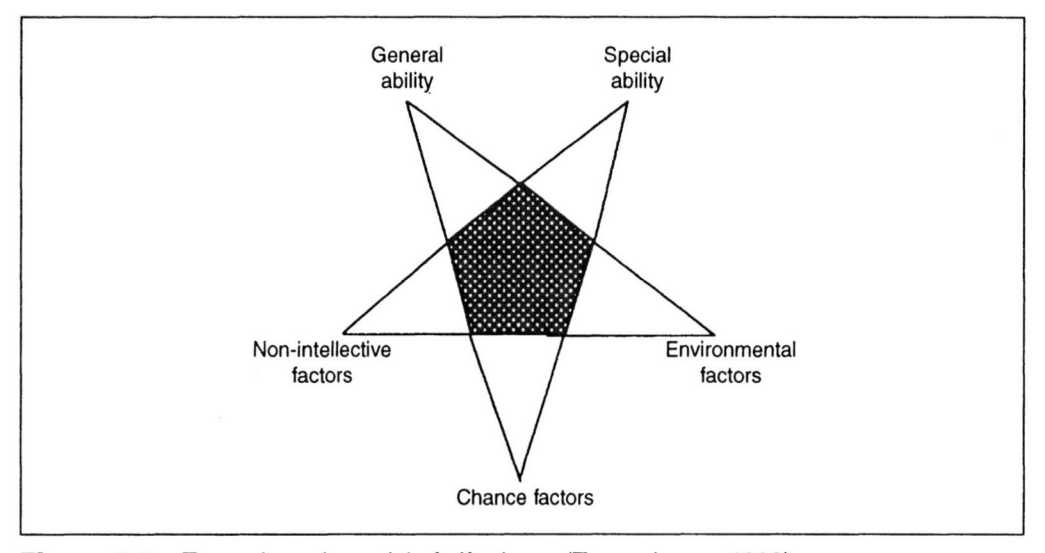

Figure 2.2 Tannenbaum's model of giftedness (Tannenbaum, 1983)

Gagné also saw the environment as being vitally important to the fulfilment of potential. This was one of the catalysts which he saw as stimulating the development of ability. While for many people ability and talent are one and the same thing, Gagné (1991) felt that the terms *giftedness* and *talent* should not be used synonymously. He saw them as two distinct concepts. For example, potential may be present but not demonstrated, while talent is the demonstration of potential.

Gagné suggested four domains in which an individual can show aptitude or demonstrate a talent: intellectual, creative, socioaffective and sensorimotor. For the development of talents, the gifted individual may use abilities derived from a number of these domains. To illustrate his theory he produced a complex model, as shown in Figure 2.3.

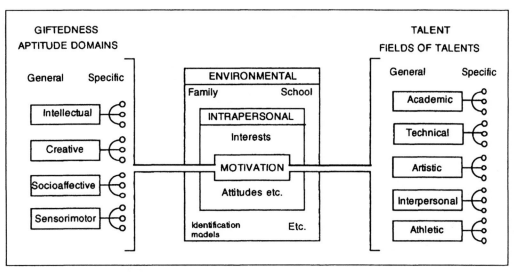

Figure 2.3   The differentiated giftedness-talent model (Gagné, 1991)

Central to his model were the environmental, intrapersonal and motivational catalysts which fostered or impeded success. A child's environment and family background, as well as his/her interests and attitudes, were seen as being vitally important to the fulfilment of potential. Unlike the Renzulli model, intellectual and creative abilities were separated. A child did not have to possess both to be designated as gifted.

This model recognised that although a child may have potential or giftedness, certain *catalysts* must be present if that potential was to be realised and translated into talent. A child with abilities may under-achieve as a result of environmental or other circumstances. Gagné allowed for this. He suggested that it is for the teacher to detect a child's potential and do all in his/her power to foster it.

So, from current thoughts on the subject, it would seem that ability involves multiple qualities, not just intellectual ones. The following section includes studies which focus on the able child, using various methods to identify them and examine influences that affect success.

The Freeman, Gross and Fullerton studies of able children

The Freeman, Gross and Fullerton studies were chosen for inclusion in this section because they focused on the early development of able children. As we have seen from the discussion of theories of intelligence, both environment and motivation are thought to have some influence on achievement. All three studies chosen for inclusion in this section support this proposal:

- The Freeman studies (1979, 1991) explored the effect that behaviour and attitudes had on achievement.
- Gross (1993) looked at the problems able children faced, particularly in school, and ways in which these could be alleviated.
- The Fullerton study (Gottfried *et al.*, 1994) focused on a comparison of gifted children and non-gifted children with regard to achievement, environment, behaviour and motivation. In particular, the authors stressed the effect that environmental factors and cognitive enrichment in the early years had on a child.

The Freeman studies

The first study was conducted between the years 1974–8 (Freeman, 1979) and considered behaviour and attitudes in particular. It involved 210 children between the ages of 5 and 14. The children had been identified as gifted by their parents, who were members of the National Association for Gifted Children (NAGC), and each child was matched with two control children. The first of the control children was matched for intelligence, although he/she was not perceived by their parents as being gifted, and the second was chosen at random. Teachers, parents and children were interviewed.

The mothers of the target children were better educated than the parents of the control children, but were less satisfied with the education they had received. Compared with the parents of the control children, they had higher expectations of their children. They described their children as having excellent memories, as being independent and as making good progress at school in comparison with the control children.

The outstanding aspect was the target children's advanced verbal ability in reading and talking. On the other hand, they were not so well-adjusted socially as the control group. The target children had few friends, preferring to play alone or with children who were older than them. Indeed this proved to be the major difference between those seen as gifted and those of equal ability but not labelled as gifted by their parents. The former were more frequently described as *difficult*. From these findings, it seemed, then, that others' perceptions of the able child, notably those of the parents and teachers, together with a child's self-concept, affected social integration. Generally, Freeman found that gifted children were at least as sound physically and emotionally as other children, but the follow-up study suggested that their future success was dependent on their social environments.

This follow-up study took place between the years 1985–8 (Freeman, 1991). Eighty-one per cent of the original sample of gifted children took part and were interviewed in their homes. If the number of A grade passes at A-level are taken as a measure of academic success, then half of the target group did particularly well. Forty-two per cent obtained between one and three A grades, and 10 per cent between four and six A grades.

A proportion of the target children studied (figures not given) were well adjusted, had adapted to adult life and were successful. However, not all of the young people had fulfilled their potential. For some, poverty had been a contributory factor to them not succeeding, while others lacked emotional support. Some felt compelled always to excel and others failed to perform under continuous pressure to do better. Inadequate educational provision was seen as partially to blame for this apparent failure to realise potential.

Of those who had attained university places, some felt that they had not been prepared for university life. In relation to this, Freeman stressed the importance of the development in young people of self-confidence and the ability to make personal relationships. Parental involvement in particular was seen by Freeman as being a catalyst for success. Those who had most influence on their children's high-level development were not those who told their children what to do, but those who engaged in the activities with them.

It was also felt that those children who had been exposed to family discord did not achieve as well as those children who had not. This is captured in the following extract:

> But that distress had not acted like the grain of sand under the shell of the oyster – none of those unhappy children looked ready to produce any pearls of art or poetry. In fact they had generally achieved less well than those of the same ability who had enjoyed peace of mind. (Freeman, 1991, p. 196)

Other causes for distress came by way of teacher 'put downs' and the influence of classmates. Both contributed to feelings of being obliged to conform to the average. Excessive pressure to achieve from both parents and teachers was also the cause of much distress. By far the greatest success was achieved when children were allowed to make their own discoveries and decisions and were afforded respect.

A child who possessed the following attributes seemed likely to succeed:

- parental support which did not put too much pressure on the child to achieve;
- freedom from domestic stress;
- the appropriate encouragement and teaching at school;
- no obligation to conform to the average but freedom to develop in his/her own way;
- encouragement to make his/her own decisions and discoveries and respect for his/her abilities.

This may be the ideal situation in which to foster the abilities of an able child and it could be suggested this is what every teacher and parent must strive for.

The Gross study

Gross (1993) evaluated the developmental histories of 15 exceptionally able young people. It was her contention that few of the children in this study had been adequately catered for educationally. She saw under-achievement as being imposed on children through the constraints of an inappropriate and undemanding educational programme. The children in this study were described by Gross as differing from their age mates predominantly in intellectual interests and academic achievement. This led to social problems and they were disliked and rejected by their classmates. It also added to existing problems of self-concept.

She advocated 'radical acceleration', i.e. placing them with children who were more than one year their senior. In this way it was intended that general self-concept and social self-concept would become stronger. This may not always be possible or desirable, however. A primary school child who was not physically as mature as classmates may feel rather out of place, particularly where games and physical education are concerned. Also the child may not be as mature emotionally as his/her older classmates.

Many children in the Gross study had difficulties exacerbated by the reluctance of schools to allow them access to other children who shared their levels of intellectual development. The children with whom they were placed did not have similar abilities or similar interests and values. This led to much unhappiness and social isolation. To maintain the approval of their peers, they had to moderate their standards of achievement and conceal their intellectual interests. Not all children succeed in hiding their ability from their peers, though, or even want to, and this study demonstrates that this can lead to great unhappiness.

Gross felt that the most effective programmes offered to children in her study had been those which had been designed with close cooperation between the school, parents and child. This suggests a fruitful way to proceed.

The Fullerton longitudinal study

The Fullerton longitudinal study (Gottfried *et al.*, 1994), aimed to look at early achievement, environment, behaviour and motivation of American children aged between birth and eight years.

The sample comprised 107 children from a wide range of middle-class families. Their development was charted from birth, and when the children were eight years old, IQ tests were administered. A cut off point of 130 on the Wechsler Intelligence Scale was used to designate a child as gifted. To avoid potential teacher bias, the children were screened and selected by tests alone. They were divided into groups, one designated by the researchers as gifted and the other non-gifted. Neither parents nor teachers knew which children belonged to the gifted or non-gifted group. Of the 107 tested, 20 were placed in the gifted range and 87 in the non-gifted group.

Evidence overwhelmingly showed that the gifted children, in contrast with the non-gifted children, were provided with more stimulating and enriched environments during their early years. In addition, the gifted children came from families with higher socio-economic status and had parents who were more highly educated than the parents of the non-gifted children. From this study, there is no evidence that parents either having a low socio-economic status or being less well educated condemn their child to under-achieve, but it does indicate that having a stimulating environment is important, however it is achieved.

The parents of the gifted also had higher aspirations for their children than did the parents of the non-gifted. In contrast, it must be said that other researchers have suggested that too much pressure to achieve can have the opposite result from that intended, as discovered by Colangelo and Dettman (1983, discussed later in this chapter).

As far as behaviour was concerned, there was very little difference between the gifted children and the non-gifted. Their level of social interaction also seemed on a par. Therefore, advantage in the cognitive realm was not associated with disadvantage in the behavioural, emotional or social aspects of functioning. Academically, the overall picture of a gifted child that emerged was that of someone who not only scored more highly with regard to academic achievement than his/her non-gifted contemporary but one who was more motivationally engaged in learning.

Although some differences in results, for example in relation to behaviour, exist between these three studies, all authors emphasised the importance of support from parents and the school in understanding the needs of the able child. For a child to be successful, parents must value education and encourage a child to work hard. In some studies, the most successful children came from families in which there was little conflict and which endorsed cultural and intellectual activities.

The dangers of labelling a child as able were stressed by Freeman since others' perceptions of the able child might set him/her apart from peers, making social integration difficult. With regard to the school, the most effective programmes of study were those designed with close cooperation between the teacher, parent and child (Gross, 1993).

So far we have considered the achieving able child. There is, however, a great deal to be said of the child who is not reaching his/her potential.

Under-achievement

An able under-achiever is one who displays a discrepancy between expected high achievement and actual performance. Such a child who will not or cannot perform at an academic level commensurate with his or her intellectual ability, as measured by IQ and attainment tests, presents a great problem to parents and teachers alike. Even at a very general level, the reasons for under-achievement are many and varied. An inadequate and unchallenging curriculum, a specific learning difficulty, social and emotional difficulties, inadequate parenting and peer pressures, can all contribute towards under-achievement and loss of potential (see for example, Freeman, 1979; Whitmore, 1980; Gleason, 1988; Emerick, 1992; Gross, 1993).

Teacher expectations can also affect achievement both positively and negatively. Winter (1993) found in almost every case that the most unfavourable expectations were associated with low-performing pupils. This raises the question of the extent to which children perform in ways that are expected of them.

Kellmer Pringle (1970) commented that the under-achieving able child is often unable to adapt to the routine of classroom life. He or she may rebel by withdrawing from classroom activities and refusing to participate in work, deliberately challenging the teacher's authority or adopting a negative attitude. By far the most common attitude, though, is:

> just doing enough to ensure that he [*sic*] will not be bothered by the teacher. As a result he is often rated average or below average but without being considered a real failure. (Kellmer Pringle, 1970, p. 110)

In this way, the under-achieving child can mask his/her problems. Perhaps another reason for under-achievement is the attitude of some teachers. Such teachers may subscribe to the commonly held view that no special educational consideration be given to able children. The argument runs that by virtue of their ability, they do not need any specialist teaching to enable them to succeed. Freeman (1991) and George (1995) found evidence of this attitude. It may be argued that able children, just like any other children, need the opportunity to extend their capabilities with appropriate teaching, and that this is vitally important.

George (1995) commented that able children are often left to get on with their work unaided because slow-learning members of the class require so much more teacher attention. This may be the case in some schools and is to some extent understandable, but it certainly does not help the under-achieving child.

There have been a number of studies conducted which consider under-achievement and we will explore these in more detail here.

The Kellmer Pringle study

An important British study which looked at under-achieving children was that conducted by Mia Kellmer Pringle (1970). She looked at the problem of why children fail at school, or are misfits. The participants were 103 children who had been referred for psychological assessment because they had some form of learning difficulty. The average age of these children was ten and a half years, they had an average IQ of 134, the lowest being 120, so they certainly should have been performing better than average.

Fewer than 50 per cent were seen by their teachers as possessing high ability.

Indeed, 84 per cent were performing at a level two or more years below their mental age in two or more basic subjects. This under-achievement was largely associated with emotional problems. These were linked to a variety of factors: strained relationships within the family; lack of peer contact; too high or too low expectations; inconsistent parental discipline.

Although these emotional difficulties were largely associated with family problems, Kellmer Pringle did emphasise the important part that a teacher plays in influencing a child. This is particularly pertinent for those children who lack appropriate role models in their own families. Kellmer Pringle believed that teachers should encourage the child and improve the child's self-concept and morale instead of merely insisting on high standards in presented work. In addition, the teacher should make parents aware of the child's difficulties and, if possible, enlist their help. In this way, she believed it possible to attain reversal of under-achievement.

The Miller study

In a more recent study, Miller (1994) also investigated children of high academic ability who were considered disruptive. In this study, conducted in the UK, it was suggested that pupils of high academic ability have motives for disrupting lessons different from those of other disruptive children who are of average or below average academic ability. A sample of Year 9 (13–14-year-old) children perceived as being disruptive by their teachers and assessed as being of high academic potential were studied in pairs with other disruptive pupils not possessing high academic potential.

Many of these children felt themselves to be frustrated academically and socially and their disruption was seen largely as a response to these problems. Much of their disruptive behaviour was associated with work. This occurred when they thought of their lessons as being unattractive. They felt that reading and writing were irrelevant to their needs in many instances and disliked listening to the teacher talking for what they considered to be lengthy periods. Also they were often bored with the tasks they were set. The same children, however, were perceived as being willing to work if they thought the tasks appropriate. This was in contrast to the disruptive children who were not seen as possessing high academic potential and who were not willing to stay on task however appropriate the work. In addition, the highly able disruptive pupils expressed a liking for teachers who talked *with* them and not *at* them. They preferred teachers who treated them as equals, or at least with respect.

Apart from these investigations, few British studies have addressed the issue of under-achievement in the able, and fewer still have considered the reversal of under-achievement. The majority of such studies have been conducted in America.

The Cupertino Project

Like Rosenthal and Jacobson (1968), Joanna Whitmore (1980) attributed under-achievement in part to low parent or teacher expectations. She suggested that this may lead to the child being under-stimulated intellectually. Low expectations may in turn foster habits of laziness and feelings of boredom. In her opinion, children learn to under-achieve as their behaviour, perceptions and attitudes are shaped by special elements and forces of the school/home experience.

She saw the first three to five years of schooling as being of the utmost importance, suggesting that it is during this time that patterns for achievement/under-achievement are set. In her opinion, one of the major factors influencing under-achievement is failure on the teacher's part to recognise a child's intellectual ability. The rigidity of the curriculum is another factor. Consequent failure to modify the curriculum to accommodate a child's needs can have long-lasting effects leading to loss of motivation because children may feel unchallenged.

Her study involved 22 children who were referred from elementary schools to become members of a special class. Teachers and school psychologists were asked to identify any student in the primary grades who had evinced, in some way, exceptionally high intellectual ability but were doing poorly in school work. The study came to be known as the Cupertino Project or the Under-Achieving-Gifted (UAG) Programme.

Whitmore (1986) reported that the project was 100 per cent successful in the initial years of the operation. Its aim was to reverse patterns of early school failure and to create highly motivated and successful individuals within two years.

The behaviour pattern of these children could be divided into two groups:

1. acute withdrawal with apparent immunity to teacher influence;
2. highly disruptive, aggressive, attention-seeking behaviour.

In either case, the child was described as a social isolate who did not know how to relate effectively to other children. Low self-esteem and high anxiety levels were other characteristics identified.

Under-achievers were grouped together for their work in order to:

1. decrease self-degrading comparisons with high achievers;
2. develop acceptance of self through acceptance of others with similar problems;
3. enjoy rewarding intellectual stimulation and a curriculum centred on their strengths and areas of past success;
4. enjoy a sense of 'genuine success' through, for example, debating, scientific experiments and so on with peers of the same advanced mental age.

The objectives of the UAG programme were to change the behaviour patterns of the child, to increase emotional adjustment and security, to accelerate socialisation and to reduce the gap between aptitude and achievement. The last was achieved by diagnosing academic deficits and learning problems and prescribing appropriate instruction to remedy the weaknesses. It was of the utmost importance that the curriculum was seen by the students to be relevant to their interests, meaningful and rewarding.

A very influential part of the evaluation process was the parent–teacher–child conference which took place at monthly intervals. During this time the previous month's work was evaluated and goals were set for the coming month. Rapid gains were achieved in language and reading, with mathematics developing more slowly. Promoting an improvement of self-esteem was deemed the most important approach to helping a child achieve. The most consistent findings were that members of the UAG class developed sturdy self-concepts, effective methods of coping with stress and social skills that generally continued to be developed and used by them.

These studies suggest that factors related to under-achievement are varied and numerous but that reversal is possible if certain intervention strategies are brought to bear and if teachers are aware that reversal is possible. This indicates that programmes focused on the individual are desirable if under-achievement is to be minimised.

So far we have considered particular studies associated with under-achievement and ways in which it can be reversed. There are, however, some specific factors which may influence achievement and these are discussed below.

Specific factors which may be associated with under-achievement

Gender

Differences in achievement patterns have been observed between boys and girls suggesting that gender can influence a child's achievement pattern. Some investigations indicate that girls achieve better results than boys, while others report the reverse.

Felouzis (1993), in her analysis of classroom interaction in France, put forward the idea that girls develop a certain interactional competence and display less rowdy behaviour than boys. It was suggested that this provided a better basis for success in comparison with boys. Undoubtedly this is not always the case, but it may be a contributory factor to a particular child's under-achievement.

Maccoby and Jacklin (1974) conducted a comprehensive review of gender differences and found that girls were superior on measures of verbal creativity after the age of seven, but that adolescent boys appear to be superior to girls in visual-spatial ability and achievement in mathematics and science. These findings were supported in an investigation by Tiedemann and Faber (1994) in Germany, and Thomas (1994) found that the pre-eminence of the girls in linguistic ability seems to continue into adolescence in England.

Thomas, who ran residential writing courses for talented children in Oxfordshire, discovered that even among pupils of equally high linguistic ability, with regard to vocabulary, syntax and secretarial competence, there was a gap between the writing performance of boys and girls. He commented:

> it is hard to resist the conclusion that girls are better writers. (Thomas, 1994, p. 154)

It appears that patterns of attainment can be associated with innate ability, but many researchers have highlighted the effect that local culture related to gender can have on achievement. These are discussed below.

A British study conducted at Thirsk School in Yorkshire found GCSE results in all subjects in 1994 showed girls achieving 12 per cent higher grades than boys, a difference slightly above the national average (Williams, 1995). It emerged that boys did not like to be seen to work too hard:

> If they do work hard, they get called a boff. At Thirsk school boff doesn't necessarily equate with intelligence, as much as diligence – and diligence isn't cool. (Williams, 1995, p. 3)

According to Williams it is acceptable (by boy lore) for boys to try hard on the football pitch because it shows they are tough. Thus boys seem more susceptible to peer group pressure than girls, especially in the teenage years. They appear to think it 'uncool' or socially demeaning to work for exams and do not like to spend time on homework. It is felt that girls do not make fun of each other in the same way that boys do, and image is not so important to them. Girls do not seem to mind staying in to do their homework. The consequences of this were reflected in the results.

In contrast, Ayles (1991) reported that highly able girls in mixed schools resent anything which sets them apart from their peers and will often, to a greater extent than boys, deliberately under-perform to achieve *normality*.

It appears, then, that local cultural influences and adverse peer group pressure, whether on a boy or girl, can lead to under-achievement. Such influences are not easy for adults to detect, whereas another particular aspect of achievement which is readily observable by others relates to poor motor control and is frequently manifested as poor handwriting.

Poor motor control

Poor motor control may seem to be a trivial problem when viewed in isolation. However, it is different if the laboriousness of the task affects concentration or is the subject of censure. Such problems are likely to result in children not achieving their full potential. Weddell (1980) found that many under-achieving children had difficulties with handwriting but that these children often displayed no difficulties with any other skills. He concluded from this that handwriting was the task which was most likely to be affected by motor organisation problems.

Congdon (1995), in a study set up to identify intellectually gifted children in North Warwickshire, found that a substantial percentage of children who were identified as manifesting high intelligence consistently failed to produce scholastic standards commensurate with their abilities. These children were often seriously under achieving in spelling, reading and sometimes arithmetic. A high proportion of these children were left handed and were in fact experiencing a degree of specific learning difficulty in the area of written language.

Fine and Pitts (1980) perceived the difficulties that under-achieving able children have with handwriting in a different light. They suggested that because of precocious language development which provoked positive attention from parents and others, the verbal arena was then likely to be identified as the one in which the child could succeed. Therefore, the child was likely to invest less energy into motor activities including sports and pencil and paper tests. This possibly has some influence on handwriting abilities, but other traits are also likely to be associated with poor motor control, for instance such children are sometimes described as being clumsy.

From this evidence it appears that children with slightly poor motor coordination may experience difficulty with handwriting. It is vitally important that children who experience these difficulties are identified as soon as possible so that their problems may be remedied. Early intervention to help with motor skills development might prevent the frustration experienced at a later stage. However, while it may be easy to identify those most severely affected, identification of mildly clumsy children at risk is not so easy. Some children may experience short-lived clumsy periods related to rapid growth and may readjust with no setbacks in other respects; others may not be so fortunate.

Poor motor control is only one of the problems with which an under-achiever may have to contend. Other factors associated with the home environment can have as much if not greater influence than those already discussed.

Marital or relationship breakdown

Marital or relationship breakdown causes a great deal of emotional stress for all concerned, including the children of the marriage. Robinson (1991), in her review of the American literature, concluded that there was converging evidence from a number of studies that, as compared with children of intact families, children of divorced parents generally experience more psychological, social and academic problems.

Mitchell (1985), who looked at the effects of divorce on children in Britain, commented on the feelings of isolation that some children experience after divorce. At school, especially primary school, some children had felt isolated from their peers, convinced that they were alone in having separated parents. She also found that parents had seldom spoken to teachers about the family situation so the teachers were unprepared for potential difficulties. It would seem that cooperation and communication between parents and teachers is vital when family discord occurs. Only if a teacher understands a child's problems can he/she help.

Heatherington *et al.* (1978) found that four-year-old American children whose families had recently experienced divorce showed marked differences in their play and peer relationships when compared with children from intact families. They were less imaginative, got on less well with peers, were more aggressive, more shy and were less frequently chosen as playmates.

These results show that behaviour and peer relationships can be affected by separation or divorce. A later study looked more closely at attainment in relation to family discord.

Stevenson and Black (1995) set out to evaluate the empirical literature about divorce in the USA. They concluded that divorce or separation can affect a child's schooling in the following ways (Stevenson and Black, 1995, p. 72):

- Offspring of divorced families receive lower scores on standardised tests and lower school grades when compared with offspring from non-divorced families.
- Offspring of divorced parents may behave less like the model student than do offspring of non-divorced parents.
- Offspring of divorced families complete fewer years of schooling than offspring from non-divorced families.
- These factors are likely to be the result of other factors such as economic problems and emotional stress.

Ferguson, Lynskey and Horwood (1994) also looked at achievement of 13-year-old children in New Zealand exposed to parental separation following the point of school entry. Their attainment scores were considerably lower than those children who had not experienced such separation. It appears that stress associated with marital breakdown may adversely affect a child's achievement, although this need not necessarily reflect diminished interest a parent takes in a child's progress. The special part parents can play in their child's achievement is discussed below.

Parental interest

Bloom (1985) described a retrospective study on world-class American athletes, musicians and scientists. It was clear in this review that parental interest and encouragement played a crucial part in individual success. The study suggested that no matter what the initial characteristics or gifts of the individuals, without a long and intensive process of encouragement, nurture and education, levels of excellence would not have been attained.

Home influences were carefully considered. It was found that the parents of achievers provided good role models; children were encouraged to do their best;

work was completed before play; disapproval was expressed when time was wasted. Extra-curricular lessons and practice were supervised by parents. They organised time, established priorities and set standards for the completion of a task. They were proud of achievements and skills and self-discipline was emphasised.

The prevailing message was that, for a gifted child to be successful, he/she must have supportive parents who valued education and encouraged their child to work hard. Little was said, though, of the parent who exerted too much pressure on their child to achieve.

There seems to be a fine line between giving a child the encouragement to succeed and putting too much pressure on him/her. Colangelo and Dettman (1983), also in America, suggested that undue pressure from parents to achieve can be a cause of under-achievement. In their review of research on parents and families of gifted children, they considered that parents who gave their children freedom, personal autonomy, support, encouragement and independence, fostered the development of ability in a positive manner.

From her extensive work with able children in Britain, Joan Freeman (1993, p. 682) summarised what good parenting entailed:

1. Parents and children should engage from birth in interaction which is positive and supportive.
2. Meaningful stimulation should be provided for children's learning.
3. A variety of experiences, which can be followed up by the child if wished, need to be encouraged.
4. Both materials and tuition with which to reach advanced heights of learning and creative production need to be available. This includes negotiating good relations with the child's school.
5. Time and experience to play and experiment are essential components.
6. Teaching skills are needed by parents to develop general and specific areas of their children's potentials.
7. Parents have to be sensitive to their child's potential talents but not try to mould them to their design.
8. Real support is not directive. Pride and pleasure in accomplishments, together with encouragement to practise, provide excellent feedback for improving performance.

The following considerations could be added to those listed above:

- Particularly in the early stages, a child should understand that great enjoyment can come through learning. The element of fun must never be forgotten.
- Judging when to leave a child to his/her own devices requires particular sensitivity on the part of the parent. A child must have time to explore on his or her own, as well as activities supported and guided by parents.

Judging the amount of support and when to provide it for any individual child is a complex skill for which there is no prior preparation and little advice available to parents. Further, some kinds of parental support are not always possible, especially if parents themselves feel inadequate in some respect. For instance, if they are unable to provide educational support or intellectual stimulation, they may reject the uniqueness of their child. In some cases a child's ability and the special attention they need from parents can cause sibling rivalry and consequently this can result in unhappiness for the whole family. Further consideration should be given by educators and researchers to advising and supporting parents of able children and their families.

Bloom's research (1985) indicated that parental encouragement is a vital adjunct to the success of the child. Nevertheless, encouragement may be perceived differently, depending on the child and the environment. What may be a stimulus for one person may be pressure to another, while what is a stimulus in some circumstances may be viewed as pressure in others. Many teachers and parents will have experienced the situation in which one sibling reacts to criticism by trying to improve while another gives up trying. Similarly the first child may respond positively to a teacher's criticism, but not to a parent's.

It has been suggested here that the causes of under-achievement are complex and are rarely found in isolation. Therefore the task for the teacher and parent is to identify and modify the events or circumstances that may cause able children to use only a portion of their ability. In addition, teachers must become skilled in tapping potential for exceptional thought, creativity, problem solving and mastery of knowledge, through teaching which stimulates, challenges and encourages these abilities.

A number of factors can affect a child's learning, as has been discussed in this chapter. However, the quality of education that a child receives may particularly affect motivation. Educational provision for the able in Britain has been considered by a number of investigators. The next chapter considers local education authority provision for the able and the surveys carried out by the National Association for Gifted Children (NAGC) in 1989 and 1995. In addition, the NAGC's research (1990 a and b) which set out to describe good practice in state and independent schools, is reviewed.

Chapter 3

Past and Current Educational Provision for Able Children

The educational provision for able children, meeting their widely varying needs, is of the utmost importance if such children are to reach their potential. The content of the National Curriculum is comprehensive enough for the basic education of the majority, but within its general provision there needs to be scope for a differentiated approach to teaching which meets individual needs. This chapter reviews educational provision for the able in Britain and the strategies employed to satisfy individual requirements.

The HMI survey on able children and associated projects

In 1992, HMI conducted a survey which focused on the education of able children in state schools. Its report was entitled *The Education of Very Able Children in Maintained Schools* (HMI, 1992).

In mixed-ability classes, differentiation was found to be essential. This involves children being set tasks at differing levels of complexity, according to their abilities. The report acknowledged the growing interest in differentiation in order to provide more appropriate levels of work for pupils across the whole ability range. In this respect the National Curriculum is important in that it emphasises the need for schools to match work with ability.

HMI found that a small number of local education authorities (LEAs) had a long-established tradition for supporting the very able. These concentrated on the development of policies and guidelines, the preparation of enrichment materials and the provision of special activities and residential courses. Schools which emphasised an enriched curriculum for all were found to be most effective in catering for very able children.

The main findings of this report are summarised as follows (HMI, 1992, pp. vii–viii):

- Very able children in primary and secondary schools are often unchallenged by the work they are set.

- Only a small core of LEAs have long-established provision for the very able but there is an increase in LEAs making specific arrangements.
- Recently there has been a concentration on an enriched curriculum for all children, not just the development of policies and guidelines.
- The most effective provision was found in those LEAs in which concerted and well-planned support had been offered to schools by the advisory or inspection service.
- Few schools had developed policies specific to the needs of the very able.
- Some schools allocated responsibility for the coordination of work with the very able to a specified member of staff, but this was not common.
- When specific attention was given to the needs of the very able, there was often a general increase in the level of expectation for all pupils.
- The schools which were most successful at challenging their very able pupils consistently sought to encourage individual effort and develop independence. The judicious intervention of the teacher to urge pupils to a higher level of knowledge, skill, understanding and thinking was crucial.

It concluded:

> In the majority of schools the expectations for very able pupils are not sufficiently high. The provision for these pupils is patchy and is not often seen as a priority. (HMI, 1992, p. 28)

It is to be hoped that since 1992 the influence of the National Curriculum, with its emphasis on differentiation and the matching of work to pupils' abilities, has been felt.

Another paper, published in the same year, highlighted the expectation that schools should provide for children of all abilities and particularly the more able (DfE, 1992).

In the following year, funds were made available to support the establishment of in-service courses for teachers who were responsible for coordinating school policy for more able children (National Association for Able Children in Education (NACE)/DfE Project). A report on this project became available in 1996 (Raffan, 1996); it described the aims of the project as follows:

- to contribute towards an improvement in overall standards in schools by raising teacher expectations of pupils generally, and able children in particular;
- to help teachers identify and make appropriate provision for able pupils.

To accomplish these aims, a series of networks around the country was planned, together with in-service courses and a series of publications for teachers covering various aspects of high ability. This was a significant step towards the recognition of able children, but it was funded for only three years. It is to be hoped that the networks set up by this project will continue to highlight the needs of the able child in years to come.

In September 1993 the DfE recommended that every school should publish a policy for very able children in its prospectus. The expectation was that policies would be turned into improved practice. It was recognised that 2–5 per cent of children may be outstandingly able and that 20 per cent may have high ability in one or more aspects of development (Dunnicliffe, 1993).

However, the shift towards Local Management of Schools (LMS) meant that LEAs had limited resources available for advisory and curriculum support services. It was possible that the number of posts linked to very able children would be further reduced. In fact in most cases (Dunnicliffe, 1993), it was left to the individual schools to decide whether or not they wished to focus on the special needs of the very able.

Such relative neglect may in part be due to the omission in the Warnock Report (1988), and subsequently both the 1991 and the 1993 Education Acts, of high ability as a category of special need. It may also be the case that terms like *giftedness, very talented* and *exceptional ability* fuel the myth that such children are born to succeed come what may. This, of course, is not guaranteed. Like all children, they need nurturing and encouragement to realise their potential. In the flurry of educational reform and change, the needs of the very able have been low on the list of priorities (Dunnicliffe, 1993).

An agency which has long been concerned with the educational provision for the able is the National Association for Gifted Children. In 1989 it conducted a survey of the provision for very able children in England, and updated it in 1995.

NAGC survey of provision

Table 3.1 summarises the main findings of the NAGC survey, which was conducted in 1989 with its findings published in 1990 (NAGC, 1990a).

Table 3.1 NAGC survey of provision

LEAs approached	105
Response	61
Those who made provision for able children	42
Named contact officer	44
Person with sole responsibility for able children	5
Able children included in the role of special needs adviser	17
No one whose responsibility included able children	20

Out of the 105 LEAs approached, 61 replied. The reason for non-returns is not documented in the report, but it is tempting to suppose that some of these remaining 44 LEAs were unable to provide data for a survey on provision for able children because it had not been collected internally. Of those who responded, 42 said that they made provision for able and talented children and 44 LEAs named a person who would act as a contact officer. (This information was to enable the NAGC to compile a register of such people.) In five of the authorities there was a designated person whose sole responsibility was the provision for able children; in a further 17 authorities, the designated person's responsibilities were for all children with special needs. In 21 of the authorities the designated person had general duties (such as inspection for primary schools). In the remaining 20, there was no one whose responsibilities included able children.

With regard to courses to help teachers identify and make provision for able and talented children, 44 of the authorities provided INSET and 53 supported the attendance of teachers on such courses.

Enrichment or extension materials for the able and talented were produced by 11 of the LEAs and 32 displayed examples of materials in a resource centre.

Of the authorities, 35 actively encouraged schools to identify able pupils but only 20 had a system for doing this. There were 47 authorities who reported conducting and supporting activities outside school hours for able and talented children.

A pattern which emerged from this data was that the authorities who had designated a person solely for the able were more likely to encourage the identification of children with high ability and to support or provide in-service training and activities outside school. Interest in the able child did increase within the next few years as the update to this survey demonstrates.

Update of provision for the able in LEAs – 1995

Of the authorities originally contacted, 80 had now provided contact names. A few of these worked directly with very able children but many more contributed through broad advisory and inspection services.

There were 39 authorities which still had not responded to the NAGC survey questionnaire and 37 of those who had responded had no policy for educating the very able. This should not necessarily be viewed in a negative light because many authorities have declared that their focus is curriculum differentiation, which encompasses the needs of the most able. There is no way of knowing from this survey, however, just how much attention is paid to the very able. The position is clearest where LEAs have stated that policies have been developed.

This report ended on a positive note:

> Schools are recognising their need to offer pupils a differentiated curriculum and many LEAs are developing strategies to help them to do so. This has helped focus attention on the curricular needs of the most able pupils as a distinct group. The drive to achieve higher standards, to meet the requirements of the revised National Curriculum and to respond to regular inspections from OFSTED are forces which are seen by our contacts as likely to maintain the momentum of this change. (NAGC, 1995, p. 3)

The organisation also conducted in-depth research into 12 schools in 1990. The ensuing report detailed what the researchers deemed to be good practice in the education of able children.

According to Their Needs — NAGC's description of good practice

Six state schools and six independent schools took part in the research conducted by the NAGC in 1990. The results discussed here are those that pertain to children between the ages of 7 and 11. The outcome was a description of good practice in the education of able children.

In all schools visited, the children appeared happy. The biggest organisational difference between state and independent schools was the staffing ratios. In the independent schools the classes were half the size of classes in the state schools.

Many teachers involved in the project felt that highly able children had a need for personal fulfilment. In order to accomplish this they had to be stretched and challenged. For part of the time they needed to be educated with children of like ability. However, to develop socially, it was felt that they needed to become fully integrated with other children in their own age range.

The appointment of a person with sole responsibility for identifying, recording and ensuring the effectiveness of provision was a major determinant of success. Visiting teachers were also felt to be important in that they provided additional expertise which was lacking at particular schools.

The resources were found to be better in preparatory schools than in state schools with regard to libraries, laboratories and sporting facilities. The preparatory schools favoured specialist teaching, particularly from the age of nine years. The curriculum was dominated by the common entrance examination, which includes French and Latin. These lessons were generally of a high academic standard. In addition, a large range of extra-curricular activities were available at the preparatory schools – for example, chess, golf, pottery.

In the state primary schools, classes were mainly mixed ability with generalist teachers. However, there were opportunities for the extension of able children through group and individualised work, together with free-choice periods.

The following seemed to have made a positive impression on the NAGC researchers and appear to be important in the education of able children:

- the high academic quality of the education provided;
- small classes;
- committed teachers and parents;
- a wealth of resources, books and facilities;
- a variety of withdrawal and extracurricular activities;
- the appointment of someone who has sole responsibility for monitoring progress and provision;

- flexibility in programming the education of the highly able, allowing for acceleration and withdrawal.

Recent developments

More recent recognition of the need for able children to be challenged is contained in the revised National Curriculum documents which came into effect in 1995. A common requirement for all programmes of study is that:

> For small numbers of pupils who may need the provision, material may be selected from earlier or later key stages where this is necessary to enable individual pupils to progress and demonstrate achievement. (DfE, 1995, p. 1)

Connected with this is the requirement contained in the *Framework for the Inspection of Schools* that inspectors look at the ways in which a school meets the needs of all pupils, whatever their ability (OFSTED, 1995).

There is no doubt that, if able children are to achieve, they must be consistently challenged. However, they must also be allowed to work at their own pace, even if this is considerably faster than the norm. This calls for flexibility in planning their curriculum requirements and versatility on behalf of their teachers. It seems desirable that one person in each school is responsible for coordinating identification, provision and records for the able. In order that this may be set in motion, a whole-school policy needs to be adopted to maintain a consistent approach. This requires a great deal of commitment from all staff. A number of authorities are now in the process of publishing advice on the teaching of able children. As an example, the following 'needs for able pupils' was taken from advice produced by Kent County Council (Kent County Working Group for the Exceptionally Able and Talented Child, 1995, p. 45).

Very able pupils need the following:
- to progress rapidly and make conceptual leaps;
- to satisfy their thirst for knowledge, which they can retain and use in different contexts;
- to have the opportunity to evaluate evidence, classify, generalise, explore alternatives, and so develop arguments in formidable style;
- to learn good study skills at an early age in order to satisfy themselves by working effectively on their own;
- encouragement in all-round development;
- challenge to their strengths almost to the point of failure;
- to be free from pressure and expectation to perform at high levels all the time.
- working contact with their intellectual peers;
- easy relations with their chronological peers, so that they are accepted into a group, to share, be useful, and learn to appreciate and learn to work with those less gifted.

If all this is to be accomplished then particular curriculum strategies are desirable if children are to receive adequate provision. Some strategies have already been tried in schools and are discussed below, while new ones may need to be created. There are a number of strategies which are used to teach the able: acceleration, enrichment and differentiation. Each has its strengths and weaknesses. Freeman (1995) commented that the American outlook favoured either separate education for the able or advancement of the children by a class or two, whereas the European preference was rather to provide a rich environment in the normal classroom.

Acceleration

Essentially acceleration means that able children experience levels of the curriculum at a faster rate than peers of the same age. Southern, Jones and Stanley (1993) have identified a range of types of acceleration including the following: early entry into school; skipping an academic year or two and therefore being educated with children who are older, or being educated with an older age group for certain subjects; subject matter acceleration, where the child is placed for part of the day with pupils who are at more advanced year levels; and continuous progress. The latter is defined as the pupil being given appropriate material for current achievement as the student becomes ready. We would call this individual differentiation.

Decisions to employ acceleration are usually made because the child learns at a faster rate than their age peers and it is thought that they will benefit from an adapted pace of instruction (Southern *et al.*, 1993). However, this policy has been criticised on the grounds that it would damage academic progress and create socio-emotional problems in those who were accelerated (Benn, 1982). Sometimes accelerated children not only find their classmates more physically mature, but also more mature emotionally. We must take care to remember that acceleration of the kind which places children with peers who are chronologically more mature may not be appropriate for every child. However, when care is taken to minimise any emotional problems, it has been found to be extremely successful (Kulik and Kulik, 1984; Gross, 1993).

Enrichment

In Britain, enrichment is possibly the most widely used strategy for making provision for the able (Montgomery, 1996). At the centre of this process is the notion that an individual child's education can be extended beyond the bounds of the normal curriculum. However enrichment is a strategy from which all children can benefit, not only the able, and should be recognised as a necessary part of education.

The terms 'enrichment' and 'extension' overlap but some researchers view them separately. Eyre and Marjoram (1990) distinguished between the two, seeing enrichment of the curriculum as meaning:

any type of activity outside the core of learning (p. 18)

and extension as:

allowing children to move through the curriculum at a faster rate either by covering it more quickly or by skipping sections. (p. 40)

For the purposes of this book enrichment and extension will be viewed in conjunction. Passow (1958) discussed guidelines for the identification of enrichment programmes. He suggested that the curriculum should be modified in three ways:

1. in the breadth or depth with which it was approached;
2. in the tempo or pace at which it was presented;
3. in the kind or content of material that was presented.

His fourth recommendation was that process skills should be developed as an essential part of the curriculum for able children.

Enrichment/extension programmes, in whatever way they are identified, should present a challenge to able children. It is this challenge that talented children usually enjoy and they delight in thinking creatively around a subject (Freeman, 1995). Ideally extension materials should be connected with ongoing work in the classrooms but should not merely be 'more material of the same kind'. The difference should be in the quality of thinking required of the task rather than the quantity of work required. It is recognised, though, that teachers have many demands on their time and the preparation of extension material is not always possible. However, there are a number of published extension/enrichment packs available to teachers (see Appendix A). Many of these projects involve children becoming intellectually involved in solving a problem, by reading and assimilating facts, selecting alternatives, thinking reflectively and arriving at a decision.

If these projects are undertaken by able children when they finish assignments ahead of others in the class, they can be helped to use their time in a worthwhile manner though the teacher will still be required to select from available packs those which best match the previous work and the work of the rest of the class.

Differentiation

The concept of differentiation was developed at a DES conference on special educational needs in 1981 (Montgomery, 1996). It involves children being set tasks at differing levels of complexity, according to their abilities.

At the DES conference, the concern was particularly about children with learning difficulties. Hegarty, Pocklington and Lucas (1981) reported that teachers in primary schools mainly adopted the strategy of teaching to the middle ability level. Any extra time was spent with the slow-learning children. The able children were either left to work unaided or were given a task similar to that already completed. The results of the work of Freeman (1991), George (1995) and Lee-Corbin (1996) support this observation.

In the 1980s, there was a trend towards individualisation of provision (Montgomery, 1996) but this was mainly with reference to children with learning difficulties. It was the National Curriculum itself which refocused attention on differentiation. It specified all children's entitlement to a broad, balanced and differentiated curriculum (Education Reform Act 1988).

Since the normal junior school class is one of mixed ability, differentiation could be viewed as being a necessity. A review by HMI on the education of very able children in maintained schools described four forms of differentiation most commonly used by teachers (HMI, 1992):

- the setting of different tasks at different levels of difficulty suitable for different levels of achievement: differentiation by input;
- the setting of common tasks which can be responded to in a positive way by all pupils: differentiation by outcomes;
- by rate of progress, allowing a pupil to progress through a course at his or her own speed;
- by enrichment, giving a pupil supplementary tasks intended to broaden or deepen skills and understanding.

Although this does provide broad opportunities for differentiation, it may not be enough for the able child whose abilities far outstrip those of the average child in the class. The report stated that differentiation by outcome meant that too often the outcome was left to the children with little guidance from the teachers. Similarly, when pupils were allowed to work at their own pace, there were few goals and little positive feedback, while the teacher concentrated on the needs of the weaker pupils. Enrichment was seen to be of value when it was planned. It can, however, be used as a way of keeping able children occupied and is often not integrated into the overall curriculum plan. Without the continuing involvement of the teacher, work was often superficial. It is accepted that teachers are extremely busy but perhaps the answer could be individual differentiation, i.e. an individual programme for a particular child (Lee-Corbin, 1996).

If provision for able children in our schools is to be of a high standard, then each task must be carefully planned. The able child does not need to repeat work for consolidation purposes as concepts are usually easily grasped (Freeman, 1991; Gross, 1993). Further, tasks set for the able child should be challenging (Montgomery, 1996). Carefully planned individual programmes, similar to those given to a child with learning difficulties, though differing in content, could be a possible answer.

Vantassel-Baska's paper in the *International Handbook of Research and Development of Giftedness and Talent* (1993) quoted the key beliefs that have guided recent curriculum theory on able education. These include the following (p. 365):

1. All learners should be provided with curriculum opportunities that allow them to obtain optimum levels of learning.
2. Gifted learners have different learning needs compared with typical learners. Therefore, the curriculum must be adapted or designed to accommodate these needs.
3. The needs of gifted learners cut across cognitive, affective, social and æsthetic areas of curriculum experiences.
4. Gifted learners are best served by a confluent approach that allows for accelerated and advanced learning, and enriched and extended experiences.
5. Curriculum experiences for gifted learners need to be carefully planned, written down, and implemented in order to maximise potential effect.
6. Curriculum development for gifted learners is an ongoing process that uses evaluation as a central tool for future planning and revision of curriculum documents.

Certainly a carefully organised curriculum, rather than a series of *ad hoc* adjustments or 'bolted-on extras', is central to the development of potential. Montgomery (1996) commented that acceleration does little more than shorten the length of time the child spends in education. The able child needs both acceleration and enrichment combined through a coherent curriculum.

Chapter 4

Portraits of the Able Child

As a member of staff in a junior school, Lee-Corbin, one of the authors, became increasingly aware that able children were not receiving the attention that they deserved. Furthermore, in many schools the needs of the able were not seen as a priority. As a special needs coordinator and as a class teacher, she was aware that special needs resources were allocated in the main to children who had learning difficulties but who were also at the lower end of the intelligence scale. This way of thinking was not peculiar to the school in which she was teaching. Colleagues from other schools, who also happened to be special needs coordinators, had reported similar attitudes and experiences. Because of their abilities, the able children were seen as capable of achieving, whatever their home/school circumstances. Therefore, in the opinion of many, they were not looked upon as meriting specialist teaching.

It became evident that this argument was flawed. Some able children failed to make the progress that was expected of them and appeared to lack motivation. Others did achieve to some extent, but it seemed that with more time and attention they could have flourished. All children need nurturing, whatever their abilities and, as a teacher, she felt it unfortunate that school resources were not fairly meted out to all children.

However, she did recognise that this experience was set in a context in which teachers' workloads had become increasingly burdensome and a great deal of teaching time had been taken up with the demands made by less able children. Because of this, the temptation was great to leave the more able to work unaided (Freeman, 1979; Hegarty, 1993; George, 1995). Although this was not to be condoned, it was at least understandable.

Thus it appeared that school resources, in the form of specialist assistance, usually went to those children who were slow learners; it seemed that a case for the needs of the able child required highlighting. Many teachers not only were pressed for time but also were unaware of the special educational requirements of the able child, for example that they need a particularly challenging curriculum if they are to achieve their full potential.

Another concern at the time was the number of able children who were not recognised as such because they were under-achieving. It was apparent that some children failed to display their talents for a variety of reasons. That these children 'fell through the net', with their potential not being recognised, was both sad and worrying. In the context in which she worked, teachers often talked about children who were highly articulate but who lacked motivation. Usually reading was of a high standard but written output was minimal. However, it was not generally felt that such children required special attention and it was school policy to allocate particular help only to those children with very specific learning needs, in particular those whose spelling and reading attainment was markedly behind that of their peers, since this was the focus of government and media attention at the time.

The question posed itself as to why some able children achieved in this particular part of England, one not generally perceived to be a deprived area, while others under-achieved. The literature on able children, summarised in Chapter 2, provided some clues about a number of factors which might contribute to achievement/under-achievement. The authors of this book also had their own theories and it was with these in mind that the research was approached.

During the time that the fieldwork was taking place (1993–4) the British educational system was undergoing a series of changes. Perhaps the biggest impetus for change was the introduction of the National Curriculum itself. Although this was embodied in the 1988 Education Reform Act, it did not become effective until September 1989. At the time of the research, teachers were inundated with paperwork related to assessment procedures and the implementation of the National Curriculum. They were attempting to manage a curriculum which was overcrowded – a situation not alleviated until January 1994 when the Dearing recommendations were implemented, resulting in the slimming down of the curriculum. Even implementing these recommendations meant coping with change. It was fortunate that headteachers and teachers found the time and energy to contribute to this investigation because it could have been viewed as merely an additional burden on top of an already burgeoning work-load. In fact all requests for information were met with courtesy and interest, demonstrating that, in spite of the other demands on their time, this issue was considered to be important by the teachers involved.

Within the context of primary education in the south of England in the 1990s, the aim of this research was to identify those factors which facilitate the translation of potential into achievement and those which inhibit such development. A review of the literature had produced a wealth of possible influential aspects but these, in general, were related to other times and other specific cultural contexts. Furthermore, they tended to be drawn mainly from the perspectives of researchers and educators focused on a particular issue or on a combination of a small number of potential influences rather than addressing the lived experience, in all its complexity, of those involved in the classroom and their 'significant others'. It was therefore important to distinguish those factors most relevant to the research aim of providing a holistic picture of the influences on the achievement of able children. The questions for this study thus became:

1. What is the lived experience of a small group of able children, their parents and their teachers, in the south of England in the 1990s, in terms of the children's achievement or under-achievement in school?
2. Which factors are generally perceived to promote or to inhibit the children's achievement?
3. What advice can be derived from the exploration of these issues for teachers and parents?

The research demanded careful design to incorporate sensitivity to all the participants' perspectives, so a number of techniques were considered and these were trialed in a pilot study.

The pilot study

This small-scale study was embarked upon in the summer term of 1993. The reasons for this were to examine testing, observation, interviewing and personal construct theory methods (see Chapter 9) to see if they were as appropriate to the research questions in practice and in context, as they were in theory. In discussion with local authority advisers, a school was suggested and the headteacher approached. She was intrigued by the aims of the project and readily agreed to the pilot study being conducted in her school. This junior school drew from a wide catchment area and included children from a variety of socio-economic groups. The following is a quotation from the researcher's fieldwork diary:

> The headteacher appeared to be very interested in the study and thought that more research should be carried out in this area, which is encouraging. The school seems to be well organised and the children well behaved, although I admit that as yet, I've only made one visit.

After discussing the study with the headteacher, two classes were selected because they included groups of highly able children. The teachers of these two classes each selected from their able groups two children to fit the following criteria:

1. one child who was achieving highly;
2. one child who was under-achieving.

All four children selected were found to score at the 95th percentile on Raven's Standard Progressive Matrices (SPM: 1991) and attained scores which placed them between the 96th and 99th percentiles on the British Picture Vocabulary Scale (BPVS: Dunn *et al.*, 1982). Two children were from a Year 5 class, aged 10, and two were from a Year 6 class, aged 11.

Outcomes of the pilot study

It was interesting to note that all the children included in this study had problems with peer relationships. This could have been because they saw themselves as being different from the other children. As an illustration of this, a comment from one of the children was:

> The other girls in my class see me as odd because I don't want a boyfriend. That's all they talk about. I want to work and pass exams and go to a university.

This affirmed the intention to observe social behaviour as well as educational activity in the main study.

One particular test, the Embedded Figures Test, (a test of perception), was used to ascertain individual responses to situations or objects based on the way each person concentrates on and absorbs new information from their surroundings. The particular way an individual carries out these processes is called the person's cognitive style. A considerable amount of research has been carried out on this particular aspect of cognitive style which is called field dependence/independence (Witkin, 1962, 1977; Saracho, 1980, 1991, 1993). Field dependence /independence (FDI) describes an individual's way of remembering, thinking and perceiving. A field dependent person tends to view their entire surroundings in a global manner, whereas a field independent person is better able to perceive individual objects independently of their surroundings.

Mismatch between a pupil and teacher's cognitive styles may affect a child's academic achievement (Saracho, 1993). One possible outcome of such a mismatch is a lower teacher expectation. This may result in the teacher seriously underestimating a pupil's academic competence.

During the pilot study it was thought to be essential to give participants a clear explanation of the aims of the test and its procedures. This was particularly the case with adults because if they felt it was in any way connected with IQ testing, they became uneasy. The teachers, for instance, made jocular comments about the test which made the researcher realise that they were feeling somewhat threatened by it. They were hastily reassured that it was not in any way connected with IQ.

Most participants found the personal construct theory method – that is repertory grids and the elicitation of constructs – an interesting activity, perhaps because of its novelty. Although the intention was to explore the unprompted perspectives of participants, it was often difficult for the researcher to withhold supplying a construct, especially with the children. This was something which had to be guarded against in the main study by practising in the interim with volunteers unconnected with the study.

During the children's interviews it was felt that some children gave socially acceptable answers and were unwilling to discuss their teachers to a great extent although they had been assured of confidentiality. Therefore it was considered that focus group interviews rather than individual ones might help the children feel less inhibited and it was decided to substitute these in the main study.

Another point which became evident during the interviews was that flexibility on the part of the interviewer was essential. One teacher interview during the pilot study took place for his convenience at 7.30 a.m. Another interview was cancelled at the last minute and rescheduled for a later date. This emphasised that an interviewer has to be prepared for small setbacks and must not become despondent.

Throughout the pilot study it became evident that the quality of the data gathered from interviews and observation gave insight into the lives of the children participating in the study. The quantitative data illustrated other aspects, concerning the measurement of abilities and, with regard to the Embedded Figures Test, different ways of thinking. This information emphasised the need for use of a range of different methods within the main study if a holistic picture of the child was to be captured.

Such detailed pictures increase the difficulty of report writing so that people are not identifiable by readers. Anonymity and confidentiality were guaranteed to the participants as part of the ethical considerations addressed in the study.

Ethics and the study

The primary consideration was that the researcher should do no harm. No participants were put under pressure to participate in the inquiry and all were treated with respect. If problems arose or concerns were hinted at, they were openly dealt with. An ethical responsibility was shown to the participants and to the schools in which the inquiry was based. This was particularly in regard to confidentiality. All identifying information such as names and locations were changed, so that participants were protected while the essence of their stories was kept intact.

Headteachers, parents and all other participants were informed of the nature of the research and written consent was sought from parents and headteachers for the children to participate. At the end of the research, a summary of the main findings and recommendations was sent to each of the schools involved and comments were invited.

Having learnt a great deal from the pilot study, the main study was planned and carried out according to the charts overleaf.

Gantt charts

Figure 4.1 sets out the time-scale of the fieldwork plan for the main study, starting in September 1993 and concluding in July 1994. Observation took place throughout the year, and the interviews also took up a large part of the year, running from January to July. As may be seen from the chart, other parts of the fieldwork, such as testing, occupied a relatively small space of time.

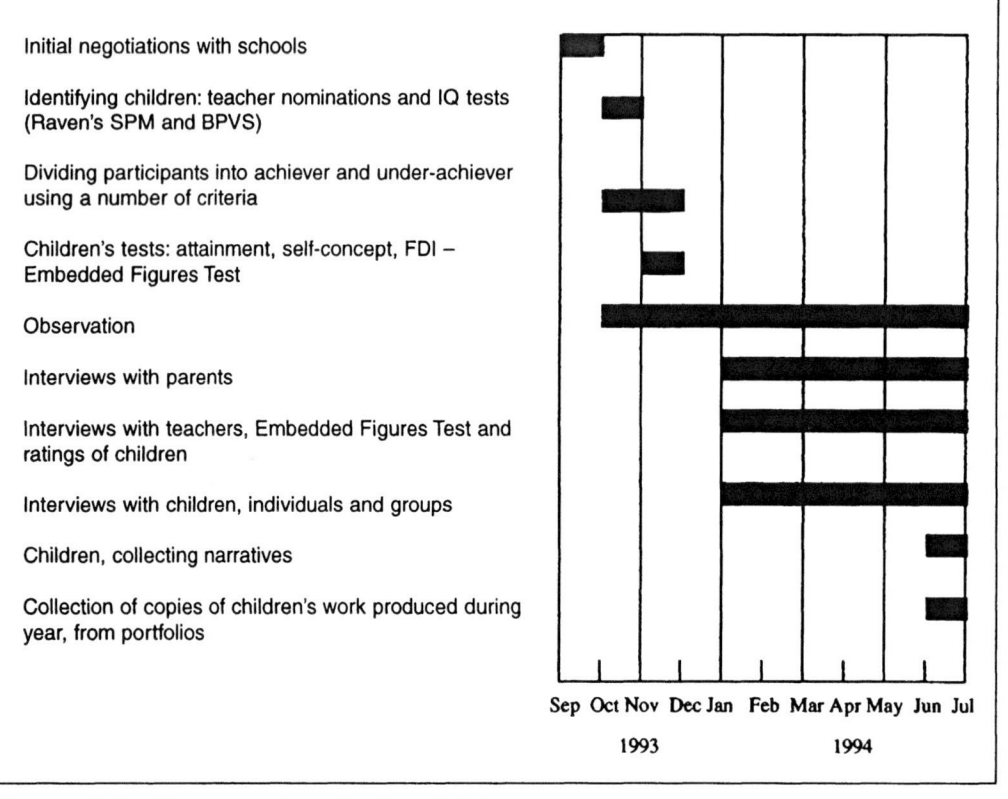

Figure 4.1   Time-scale for collection of data

Figure 4.2 presents the time-scale for the analysis and synthesis of the data. It includes the literature review, which continued throughout the research and is ongoing.

Selection of schools

As may be seen from Figure 4.1, the selection of schools was made in September 1993. From the literature, it was suggested that different socio-economic backgrounds may have some effect on a child's performance in school. For example, poverty in a family can affect a child's achievement pattern adversely (Hitchfield, 1973; Freeman, 1991; Gottfried *et al.*, 1994). Thus it was thought that three schools in the same geographical area which had different social intakes would be appropriate for the study. Advice was sought from local authority advisers about which schools demonstrating this range would be amenable to research on able children. Three headteachers were approached by letter, which set

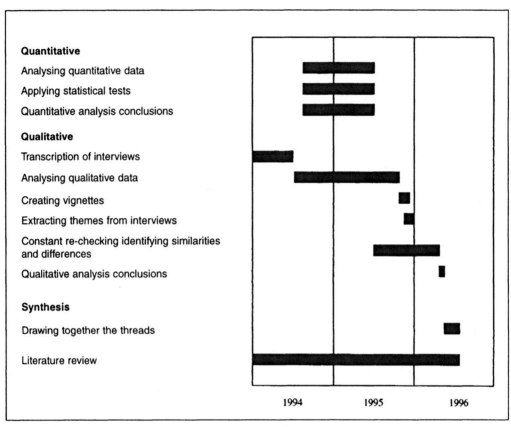

Figure 4.2 Time-scale for analysis and synthesis

out the aims of the research, the age of the children who should be involved and the duration of the study. Unfortunately one headteacher decided that he did not want his school to be involved. Another similar school was suggested by an adviser and the headteacher of this school agreed to take part. The letters were followed up by a visit and the plan of the research discussed with the headteachers and teachers who were to be involved.

In all schools the headteacher proposed the teachers who would participate but, as it had been stipulated that children from Years 5 and 6 were required, teacher choice was limited. However, without exception, all teachers appeared interested in the project and eager to take part. In one school (School A), a teacher coordinated meetings with other teachers and children. For goodwill reasons these procedures were not challenged, since it was expected they would make little difference of consequence to the research process. The next step was to contact parents to gain permission for their children to become participants and also to ask if the parents would take part in interviews. The aims of the research were carefully set out so that the parents knew exactly what their child would be involved with.

One headteacher felt that he would prefer to contact the parents in his school himself (School A), but the other headteachers were happy to let the researcher write to the parents. The majority of responding parents were pleased for their children to be involved in the study and very few refused their permission – in fact, only two parents out of 56. Acceptance of invitations to take part in parental interviews was also encouraging from two schools, Schools B and C. All parents from Schools B and C agreed to be interviewed, but for two of these parents communication was difficult and eventually no time was arranged for interviews, although every attempt was made to facilitate them. No acceptances were received for parental interviews from school A, although the parents gave their consent for their children to take part in the research. It seemed politic not to pursue this issue any further since it was clear that the notion of the parent interviews caused the headteacher some discomfort. This highlights the tension between pursuing the capture of all relevant data and remaining sensitive to the needs and perspectives of participants in research.

Selection of children

From the three schools included in the study, 12 teachers in all were asked to select children whom they considered to be able. Fifty-four children were chosen and these were divided into two groups designated achievers or under-achievers by their teachers. Further selection was then carried out using scores on intelligence tests. It was felt that the intelligence tests employed should not place too much emphasis on linguistic ability as children from one of the schools taking part could possibly be at a disadvantage given the varied cultural background of the catchment area. The Raven's Standard Progressive Matrices (SPM: Raven, 1991), and the British Picture Vocabulary Scale (BPVS: Dunn *et al.*, 1982) were consequently used to give a non-verbal and verbal intelligence score respectively.

Children whose scores were at the 90th percentile level or above on either of the tests were then finally chosen to take part in the study. These selection procedures were applied across the whole of the sample and quite fortuitously led to approximately equal numbers from each of the schools. This selection yielded 11 children from School A, 11 children from School B and 12 children from School C. With regard to those children who were deselected by the intelligence test, although they had been selected by the teachers, there were none for whom their teacher's judgement had been widely misplaced. On the other hand there were some who fell slightly short of the 90th percentile, and it was felt that the criterion for including the top 10 per cent of the ability range should be adhered to.

Teachers were asked to rate the children as achievers or under-achievers according to criteria supplied by the researcher, who in turn drew on guidance from the literature. These were as follows:

The achievers exhibited all or most of the following traits:

- in general classwork, the child achieves at a level well above the average expectation level for that year group;
- generally work is complete and well done;
- he/she has superior comprehension and retention of concepts;
- he/she is articulate and this command of English is shown in written work.

The under-achievers exhibited all or most of the following traits:

- in general classwork, the child achieves at or below the average expectation level for that year group;
- he/she frequently hands in work that is incomplete or poorly done;
- he/she has superior comprehension and retention of concepts when interested;
- he/she exhibits a vast gap between oral and written work.

The researcher's experience as a primary school teacher was brought to bear at this point. The written work of each child was examined closely and an agreement was reached between the teacher and researcher as to the allocation of children to the 'achievers' or 'under-achievers' groups. This yielded eight achievers and three under-achievers from School A; five achievers and six under-achievers from School B; and five achievers and seven under-achievers from School C.

Intelligence tests, tests of attainment (e.g. for reading and mathematics) and other psychological tests, including a test to determine self-concept, were used, but the main part of the research was based on interviews, observation and personal construct psychology techniques.

Interviews

Interviews took place over a six-month period, as may be seen from Figure 4.1. Each interview was approached in a semi-structured manner. There were issues to be probed but the ordering of these, and the asking of additional questions which arose from the responses made, were left to the interviewer. This approach was thought appropriate as it was desirable to retain flexibility and to allow the interviewee the freedom to bring up topics which were significant to him/her.

Most parents were interviewed in their own homes as it was felt that they would feel more secure and able to relax in familiar surroundings. Also it gave the researcher a view of family life. All of the interviews conducted at home took place in the family's sitting room. This provided a pleasant atmosphere for both interviewer and respondent. The majority of parental interviews were with the mothers of the children involved, although the fathers were encouraged to take part. In many cases the work of the latter took up a great deal of their day and they had very little leisure time; other fathers felt it was more appropriate for their wives to be interviewed, possibly because the mothers were more directly involved with the everyday nurturing of the child.

Questions centred around the following topics:

- Early development.
- Early learning ability – e.g. the age at which they read.
- School subjects favoured by the children.
- Vocabulary.
- Their personality, including self-esteem.
- Educational provision.
- Relationships with the school staff.
- Interests.
- Concentration and attention skills.
- Memory and imagination.
- Self-discipline and attitude towards criticism.
- Attitude towards school.
- Ability to socialise.
- Parental expectations.
- Relationships within the family.

These topics were explored in all interviews but not necessarily in the above order. The interviewee was always free to introduce topics of his/her own choice and often did.

All teachers were interviewed at their own schools. The interviewer had little say in where the interviews took place since it was, as with the parents, the teachers' home ground. Most frequently, these took place either during the lunch break or after school in classrooms, which were seen as places where there would be the minimum disruption. If there was an area in the classroom where the seating arrangements were fairly informal – for example a reading corner – then this was suggested by the researcher as the place where the interview should take place. Otherwise the children's tables were used in preference to the teacher's table. This served to put the teacher and researcher on an equal footing and to make the teacher feel more relaxed. General topics of conversation were introduced to facilitate the establishment of rapport before questions were posed. The interviews centred around the following topics:

The teacher
- The teacher's idea of an able child.
- Experiences they encountered with able children.
- Their relationship with parents.

The children
- Social skills.
- Concentration and attention.
- Vocabulary and English skills.
- Other academic abilities.

- Creativity.
- Self-discipline and organisation.
- Personality and self-esteem.

Like the parents, the teachers were encouraged to talk about anything which they thought would add to the portrait of the child being studied.

Interviewing the children themselves was an important aspect of this research because it gave the children voice. It was felt to be important that the children were not interviewed in the classroom so that they would not feel that they were being interviewed by a member of staff. Every effort was made to make them feel at ease and they were reassured about confidentiality. Interviews usually took place in the school library where the seating was comfortable. The library was the place where they were trusted to work occasionally and there they were not under constant supervision. This made it an ideal place to conduct such interviews because it was associated with freedom and trust.

Focus interviews usually comprised three or four children to a group. In particular it helped the more self-conscious children to talk about their own feelings and interests. A general discussion about hobbies and favourite school subjects served to open the interview and to put them at their ease. In this way rapport between interviewer and respondents was established. The contrast between the group interviews and the individual interviews was very marked. The children became quite uninhibited during group discussions and gave their opinions freely. With their peers around them to give support, they became more relaxed when answering questions. In this situation, the children challenged each other, were willing to discuss their teachers and many new topics were considered.

Topics planned for discussion were as follows:

- Academic subjects enjoyed or liked.
- Whether or not work was planned just for them or the whole class.
- Whether or not they had the opportunity to follow their own interests with regard to academic work.
- What they thought of school work.
- The sort of teachers they liked.
- Whether they had a lot of friends or not.
- Interests outside school.
- Reading habits.
- Whether they always tried hard to do their best.

A quotation from the fieldwork diary is as follows:

Of all the techniques which I've used to date in this study, I think interviewing has been the most enjoyable. All the people interviewed have been so eager to take part and have shown me snippets of their lives which I've felt privileged to see.

Personal construct theory – the repertory grids

An important aspect of this study was the attitude the teacher had towards his/her pupils and also the way in which the pupil perceived the teacher. In order to discover whether the attainment of children was affected by teacher attitude, it was necessary to find some means of measuring personal perceptions or constructs. Kelly's personal construct theory provided a powerful tool for this, in the form of repertory grids used to elicit constructs (see Chapter 9).

Kelly introduced his theory on personal constructs in a book entitled *The Psychology of Personal Constructs* (1955). The book centred on the individual's perception and understanding of his/her environment and people in it. Personal constructs are the dimensions that an individual uses to make sense of aspects of his/her daily life and it is suggested that each of these is a continuum, described by two poles – such as cheerful >>>> miserable – along which people or events can be placed. A person's repertoire of constructs is explored by using a repertory grid. This method was used to ascertain personal constructs of teachers to evaluate whether they assist or hinder achievement in children since constructs orientate behaviour (for example neat and poor presentation could be two poles of a construct for a particular teacher and this could influence the way that teacher views children). It was employed with pupils to determine personal and organisational aspects which to them described a good teacher.

This technique had been successfully employed by a number of researchers (e.g. Nash, 1973; Pope and Keen, 1981), who saw personal construct theory as being especially useful in classroom research. Nash (1973) in particular related the behaviour of pupils to teachers' perceptions of them. Favourable and unfavourable perceptions of the children on the part of the teachers gave rise to different behaviour.

Teachers were asked to complete a repertory grid after being interviewed. The children also completed their repertory grids individually, after an interview. As with the interview, it was felt to be essential to reassure participants of confidentiality and to define the purpose of repertory grids. It was through personal construct psychology that it was hoped to discover more about the nuances of meaning in pupil–teacher interaction. At the time this part of the research was conducted the researcher commented in her diary:

> Both teachers and children seem genuinely interested in rep. grids. The teachers seemed pleased with the opportunity to reflect on what they thought about able children and the children delighted to be able to discuss their teachers in a personal way.

The teachers were asked to include in their repertory grid six able pupils in their class, incorporating those who were participants in the study. The pupils were asked to think of five or six teachers who had taught them. For some children the number was smaller, particularly if they had attended a small school previously and had been taught by the same teacher for two consecutive years.

Care was taken not to impose constructs although help in 'splitting entwined constructs' (Pope and Denicolo, 1993), was given. At times this was difficult to uphold, particularly with the children, but it was felt that a truer picture could be obtained if free elicitation of constructs was conserved initially, even if they were discussed and refined later. For example:

understanding >>>> shouts a lot

was split to provide two constructs. These were:

understanding >>>> doesn't listen to problems

and

talks quietly >>>> shouts a lot.

It was through repertory grids that it was hoped to discover more about the attitudes that pupils and teachers held regarding each other and life within the classroom. Observing classroom life also gave insights into feelings that pupils and teachers had towards each other.

Observation

During interviews, it was the participants' perceptions that were explored but during observation, the researcher was able to add a further perspective to the picture. The impressions and feelings of the observer became part of the data. Observation took place over a period of a year both before and after the interviews. It accessed different sorts of data from that of interviews. Often it illuminated comments which had been made during the interviews. Conversely, observed behaviour formed the basis of some questions within interviews and thus was elaborated on during an interview.

The aim was not to conduct a highly structured observation but to observe the natural interactions between pupils and their teacher as well as those between peers. In addition, the behavioural indicators of children's attitudes towards the work they were set was observed. In this way, the general ambience of the classroom was perceived and noted.

When observation first began, the role of a visiting onlooker was adopted. Over time, as the children became used to the researcher being in the classroom, her presence became accepted and a rapport was built up between researcher and children. Care was taken though, in providing any practical help, that the general level of interaction and tone within the classroom was not unduly influenced.

The children were observed in the playground as well as in the classroom because it was recognised that people's behaviour may vary in different settings. However, in this fieldwork, features most salient to the classroom interactions were focused on, such as interaction with peers and how 'free time' was occupied. The diary entry after a period of observation was:

> This week I've been able to see the problem from both the children's and the teachers' points of view. Possible explanations for certain actions e.g. irritation on the part of the teachers for a child's lack of attention and a child's frustration because s/he had not been able to get time with the teacher became apparent. A circular problem?

Children's narratives

Four achieving children and four under-achieving children were chosen for in-depth case studies from the sample interviewed, balanced between boys and girls. These children were asked to provide narratives describing the high and low points of their lives for incorporation into vignettes. To enable the researcher to form as complete a picture as possible, it was important that the parents of the children selected had also been interviewed. In addition, it was felt desirable that each child should present a contrasting picture. In this way, the vignettes would be representative of the divergence of personalities and achievement patterns exhibited by the group as a whole.

As the narratives were to be completed in the children's own time, some were more substantial than others. One child (Fergus) asked if he could record his narrative using a tape recorder and this was readily agreed to. This was transcribed verbatim. The diary entry at this time was:

> there was a great difference in the way the narratives were presented. One child talked of her 'memoirs', another made his narrative appear like a radio documentary ... 'this is Fergus signing off ...'

The narratives could be considered as one example of the children's work but it was felt to be important to collect samples of work from all children to allow comparisons to be made. It was important for the researcher to look at the children's work so that any comments given on the quality of the work set and on the calibre of the response should be accurate.

Personal perspective at this stage

Although it had been frustrating at times (e.g. interviews and observation sessions cancelled at short notice), the collection of data was possibly the most rewarding part of the research. Perhaps it was the contact with people who were eager to talk about children of high ability and working intensively with such children, which made it so.

The amount of data collected at this stage was rather overwhelming. Interviews were transcribed soon after they were conducted so that particular impressions, which were fresh at the time, should not be lost. Analysis was left until the following academic year. This was advantageous in that it permitted immersion in the data and also allowed a time for reflection; a chance to stand back and look for patterns without being distracted by the normal day-to-day interactions with participants and the highs and lows in their lives, all of which might have influenced possible interpretations.

The following is a quotation from the fieldwork diary at the end of the data collection period:

As the fieldwork drew to a close, it was with mixed feelings that I prepared to leave these individuals with whom I had built up a relationship. That the intensity of the work was over was a relief but I felt that I had been honoured to be allowed a glimpse of the lives of my participants. However, such was the relationship between myself and the participants that I was encouraged to do justice to their efforts by analysing and interpreting the data provided with rigour and honesty.

Chapter 5

Emerging Issues

As was suggested in the last chapter, it was important to do justice to the participants by undertaking a thorough analysis of the data they had provided. In this chapter we focus on the formal analysis of the results – the general data as it related to all the children – before going on, in the next chapter, to show what it meant for individual children. The analyses of both parts of the data – quantitative (testing and factual information) and the qualitative (interviews, children's narratives, observation, repertory grids) – took over a year and were found to be supportive of each other. The issues connected with the quantitative analysis are summarised in the following table and each is discussed in turn thereafter, with references provided to how these relate to those described in earlier chapters.

Table 5.1 Significant factors associated with achievement

Handwriting
Family stability
Socio-economic status
Self-concept
Teacher expectations
Gender
Field dependence/independence
Number of schools attended
Appropriateness of work
Cooperation between home and school
Emotional problems
Parental expectation/support
Undetected specific learning difficulties

Quantitative analysis

Handwriting

The comparison of the achievers and the under-achievers revealed a number of differences. One of the findings was that non-fluent handwriting was related to under-achievement. Teachers were asked to assess the handwriting of each child and to give a National Curriculum level to each.

The explanation for the grading is as follows:

Level 2 – letters accurately formed and consistent in size.
Level 3 – handwriting is joined and legible but not fluent.
Level 4 – handwriting is fluent, joined and legible.

By the end of Key Stage 2, i.e. by 11 years, the writing should be within the range of Levels 2–5 (DfE, 1995). The children deemed to be non-fluent handwriters were seen to be working at Levels 2 or 3, while fluent handwriters had attained Level 4.

Table 5.2 Achievement and under-achievement compared with handwriting fluency

NC handwriting level	Achievers	Under-achievers
2	0	4
3	1	7
4	17	5

As can be seen in Table 5.2, the number of achievers who were writing at Level 4 was far greater than the number of under-achievers writing at that level. When the numbers of achievers and under-achievers are compared in terms of fluency of handwriting, the differences are found to be statistically significant. Fluency of handwriting seemed to go hand in hand with achievement in all three schools (see Figure 5.1).

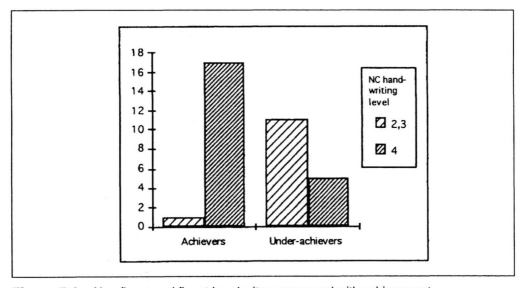

Figure 5.1 Non-fluent and fluent handwriters compared with achievement

Congdon (1995), in a study which was set up to identify intellectually gifted children in North Warwickshire, found that a substantial percentage of children identified as manifesting high intelligence, but who consistently failed to produce scholastic standards commensurate with their abilities, were in fact experiencing a degree of specific learning difficulty in the area of written language.

It is interesting to note that weak fine-motor control and poor hand-to-eye coordination have been considered by Gardner (1994) to be indicators of dyslexia. Intellectual ability does not necessarily mean mastery over the pen, but dyslexia is very difficult to diagnose and may have been overlooked in the schools.

The emotional frustration of having a lot to say and not being able to write it down must be very thwarting. Certainly any learning disability can lead to feelings of inadequacy. This may in turn result in disruptive behaviour or withdrawal, as noted by Emerick (1992). If handwriting scores are compared with attainment scores, the fluent handwriters score more highly than the non-fluent writers for mathematics which requires written work. Interestingly there was no significant difference, though, when reading attainment scores – which require no writing skills – were compared between fluent and non-fluent handwriters. This supports the proposition that difficulties in writing can disadvantage pupils who would otherwise be considered as able.

Family stability

A high proportion of under-achievers in this study were from homes where marital breakdown had occurred. Although such breakdown is not uncommon, the emotional effect that this has on a child must not be under-estimated. Although one would expect marital breakdown of parents to affect achievement (Mulkey *et al.*, 1992; Plante *et al.*, 1993; Ferguson *et al.*, 1994), the number of under-achievers from such homes compared with the number of achievers was particularly striking.

Under-achievers
- 9 children came from families which had experienced marital breakdown.
- 7 children came from families where this had not occurred.

Achievers
- 1 came from a family which had experienced marital breakdown.
- 17 came from families where this had not occurred.

The differences between the two groups were statistically significant (see Figure 5.2).

Various studies have illuminated this problem; for instance, Gleason (1988) was of the opinion that emotional disturbance was the single most common cause of under-achievement. Also, the amount of time which a parent has to spend with a child and their commitment to family life is often reduced when a divorce or

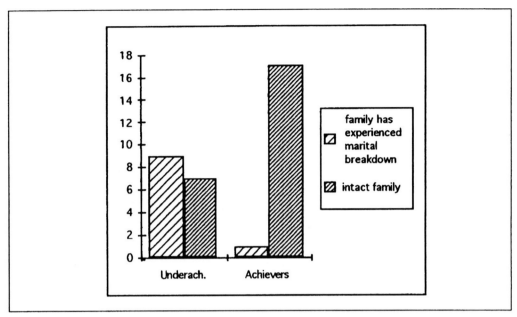

Figure 5.2   Family breakdown compared with achievement

separation occurs. McLanaghan (1992) indicated that there is no definite proof that divorce itself causes lower attainment, but perhaps because a single parent has more commitments, the attention a child receives may be less than before the family breakdown.

Weisner and Garnier (1992) believed that strong commitment to meaningful values regarding the importance of one's family lifestyle can protect children. Even if a child does live with just one parent, but has a stable family life and support with their education, then he/she may still achieve. It must also be noted in passing that some children may be in a more stable emotional environment after divorce or separation has occurred because there is no longer discord in the family (Weisner and Garnier, 1992).

Socio-economic status

Information was obtained about the occupation of the principal wage earner in each family, since this gives a good indication of the socio-economic status of the family. The bulk of the achievers in this study were concentrated in the socio-economic groups A and B (1 and 2), although the under-achievers seemed evenly spaced throughout the groups.

The Registrar General's classification of occupations is as follows:

A   Professional occupation.
B   Intermediate occupation (managers etc.).

C1   Skilled occupation.
C2   Partly skilled occupation.
D   Unskilled occupation.

These socio-economic groups are sometimes numbered 1–5 for groups A–D. The occupations in groups A and B are generally regarded as non-manual and those in groups C2 and D as manual.

Thus the socio-economic status of parents seemed to be closely associated with achievement/under-achievement (see Figure 5.3). With reference to the Registrar General's classification of occupations, the pupil distribution in the sample was as follows:

Groups A + B   12 achievers.
                   5 under-achievers.

Group C1   6 achievers.
                   6 under-achievers.

Groups C2 + D   no achievers
                   5 under-achievers.

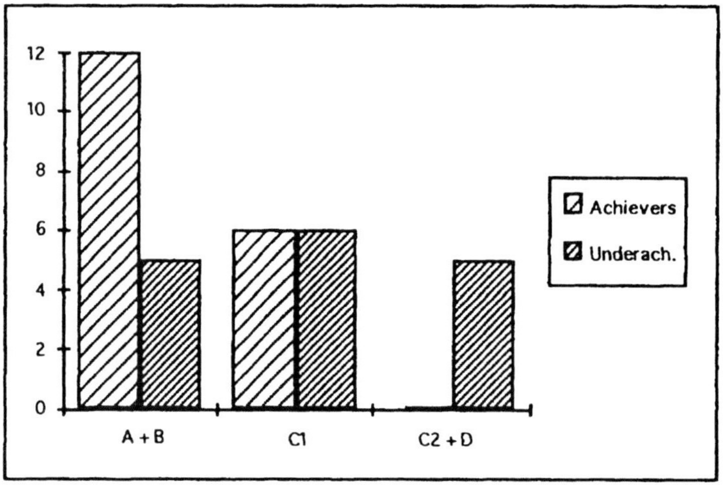

Figure 5.3   Achievement compared with occupation

The differences in the numbers of achievers and under-achievers between the groups was statistically significant. Groups A and B had the largest number of achievers – in fact twice that of group C1 – while groups C2 and D had none at all. The under-achievers, however, seemed evenly spaced throughout the groups, with group C1 having a slightly larger number. For mathematics attainment, there was a statistically significant difference between the groups (if A and B were grouped together and C and D were also taken as a single entity) with the A and B group scoring significantly higher than the C and D group. No difference was found however, with regard to reading. Freeman (1979) found that middle-class parents were more involved with their children's education and gave more time and encouragement to them than working-class parents. This could be one explanation for these results.

It appeared that the parents of the majority of the achievers had better-paid jobs. A higher socio-economic status could indicate a richer lifestyle for the children – for example a good diet, the availability of books in the home, visits to places of interest. A child from a poorer background might find some or all these lacking. These results, therefore, mirrored those reported in the Fullerton Study (Gottfried *et al.*, 1994) which found that the able children came from families with higher socio-economic status and had parents who were more highly educated than the less able. However, the fact that under-achievers were evenly spaced throughout the groups in this study points to the possibility that factors other than socio-economic status contribute towards under-achievement. In other words, although able children are found in each socio-economic group, and although some factors leading to under-achievement are relevant to all groups, able children in groups C and D seem to be especially at risk.

Other family-related factors

In this study, parenting style (i.e. whether it was authoritarian, child-centred or a mixture of the two), a child's position in the family and whether or not a parent had received higher education did not appear to be associated with achievement. There was a difference in parental ages at the birth of the participating child between two of the schools. The mean age for parents at the birth of their child at one school was 33 whilst at the other the mean age of parents at the birth of their child was 26. There was also a difference in mean attainment scores between these two schools. This may suggest that an older parent with greater experience would be more supportive with regard to education, but it could be that these correlations have no causal similarity.

Self-concept and interactional competence

Considering self-concept scores, generally no difference was found between the achieving and under-achieving children, thus contesting suggestions by Covington (1984) and Whitmore (1988) that under-achieving children had a lower self-concept than achieving children. However, the subjects in which the achieving children scored more highly than the under-achievers were drama and social awareness. It seems likely that the achievers had acquired a higher level of interactional competence and that this could be affecting them positively. It could also have an effect on how the teacher perceives them and consequently interacts with them.

Teacher expectation

Comparison of the self-concept scores and teacher rating scores generally showed that the teachers' estimates of the abilities and aptitudes of the pupils who were achieving were significantly higher than those of the pupils' estimates. This included pupil and teacher assessment of appearance. Perhaps the achieving children also matched the teachers' visual model of able children. Similar results were found for presentation and concentration with the achievers scoring highly in the teachers' estimations. As the teachers' opinions of the achieving children were generally high, then it would be logical to assume that their expectations were high also.

Thus, high teacher expectations could be affecting the achievers in a positive manner, whereas the reverse may be true for the under-achievers. This matches the findings of Winter (1993), who discovered that in almost every case the most unfavourable expectations were associated with the low-performing pupils. This raises the question of the extent to which children perform in the way that is expected of them. Rosenthal and Jacobson (1968) claimed that performance and attainment in school subjects was significantly improved when improvement was expected. Perhaps the achieving children fall into this category. Such an effect is in the nature of self-fulfilling prophesy – when you do badly, others come to expect this of you, and you respond to meet their expectations in a downward spiral. The contrast is when you are expected to do well and your behaviour rises to the occasion.

Gender

No statistically significant differences were discovered between girls and boys in terms of their distribution within schools, handwriting, self-concept and reading and mathematics attainment scores. However, in the self-concept and teacher ratings, it was observed that teachers rated girls more highly than boys and, in addition, rated the girls more highly than the girls rated themselves. Both results were statistically significant. With regard to achieving and under-achieving children, the results indicated that boys were indeed more likely to under-achieve than girls. Although the result was not statistically significant, the trend was suggestive of this. A number of studies have noted similar results (Mboya, 1993; Warrick and Naglieri, 1993; Flynn and Rahbar, 1994). Felouzis (1993) put forward the idea that girls develop a certain interactional competence and display less rowdy behaviour than boys which, it was suggested, provided a better basis for success. In conjunction with teachers' expectations of achievement, the influence of social competence should not be ignored, for each may affect the other.

Field dependence/independence

As was discussed in Chapter 4, field dependence/independence (FDI) is a dimension of cognitive style describing an individual's way of remembering, thinking and perceiving. In this study the interaction between a child's and teacher's FDI appeared not to be associated with achievement. Neither style was particularly associated with degrees of achievement. Saracho (1991, 1993) implied that a mismatch in FDI orientation between teacher and child could lead to under-achievement. Similarly, when a child and teacher have a preferred cognitive style in common, then the child's achievement could be enhanced. In this investigation, FDI did not appear to be related to achievement/under-achievement. Only a small number of teachers took part in this study and the majority were 'field independent'. The lack of relationship between pupil and teacher FDI and achievement may therefore be a product of the peculiarity of the sample rather than indicating that no such relationship might exist on a statistically large scale.

Number of schools attended

Information was collected on how many schools each child had attended and it became apparent that children who had attended more than two schools were more likely to under-achieve in mathematics than those who had attended fewer schools. Such results were also noted by Douglas (1969), Firth (1974), Glaister (1976) and Lee-Corbin (1984). There could therefore be a link between the number of schools attended and achievement, and further research on a larger scale may be useful in evaluating this link. Caution must be exercised here, though, as children who have moved school frequently may have done so for a number of reasons which have already been considered, such as marital breakdown.

Qualitative analysis

As the interview data were examined during the analysis stage, several themes began to emerge and some were thought to be related. Table 5.3 sets out the themes discussed and a selection of these, together with comments from teachers, parents and children, are included in the following section.

Comments of the participants are summarised in the boxes at the beginning of each section, giving the reader an overall impression before presenting salient transcript details.

Table 5.3   Significant qualitative factors associated with achievement

• Appropriateness of work	• Self- and social esteem
• Lack of specialist teachers	• Emotional problems
• Cooperation between parents and teachers	• Social skills
	• Competition
• Importance of parental knowledge of the education system	• Handwriting
	• Attitude towards school
• Courses for teachers	• Expectations

Appropriateness of work

Achievers		
Parents	**Teachers**	**Children**
• Lack of stimulation • Disillusioned at lack of provision • Not extended enough • Lack of homework has made child lazy	• Feel that the achievers are stimulated and that the work they do is appropriate	• Not a lot of criticism from the achievers, although a few think that some work set is boring and some dislike repetition

Under-achievers		
Parents	**Teachers**	**Children**
• Lack of appropriate work associated with dearth of stimulation • Teacher must find ways of interesting child and making him/her work • Child's dislike of repetition • More opportunities for able children to work together • Question whether enough core work covered • Children need to be given confidence	• Child has short attention span • Child doesn't listen to instructions • Child needs constant monitoring • Child talks too much • Child doesn't fit in • Child has to be centre of attention • Child doesn't conform	• Bored with written work • Told to repeat work because it's poorly presented • Would prefer to do different work, not to be given more of the same • No time to think; accused of wasting time if not writing

Many children, both achievers and under-achievers, complained to their parents that when they finished their work in class they were often asked to complete another piece of work which was similar. They also often told their parents that their work was too easy. In relation to this aspect of their children's school experience the parents of the achievers did have some criticisms to make. One parent was disillusioned with the education her child was receiving, the inappropriate work her child was set and the general lack of provision for able children. The following extract from her interview demonstrates this concern:

> I have taken Harriet to our GP because she has been very depressed and she has had all sorts of minor things wrong with her because she didn't want to go to school. He [the doctor] felt that this stemmed from her not being provided for at school.

Conversely, there were parents of achievers who were satisfied with the education their children were receiving from whichever school they attended, as the following quotation implies:

> I've had three children go through School B and they've all been helped in different ways. Generally we've been pleased. They give them a good all-round education. They've certainly stretched Gary.

Generally the parents of the under-achievers were more vociferous about inappropriate work. One of the main causes for concern was lack of stimulation:

> Children like Toby should be stimulated and taken that step further.

Parents thought that teachers should be able to encourage their children to work. They also thought that tasks should be centred around a child's interests, as Alistair's mother expressed:

> Work needs to be done on Alistair's social skills and concentration skills. Then he'll be able to cope with the stress of life. Also he needs to be channelled more into things he's interested in.

On the other hand, teachers were aware of some problems but viewed them differently. For instance teachers reported that many of the under-achievers had short attention spans:

> Alistair has a very limited attention span, unless it's something he's interested in. It's worst of all when we're sitting on the carpet [discussing]. He has to be centre stage.

The majority of achieving children had few complaints about their work. However, some of them disliked repetition:

> Sometimes we have to do work we already know. That's when it gets boring.

The under-achieving children, many of whom had poor handwriting, reported being bored with written work, mainly because they had been told that it was messy and it had to be repeated. A typical remark was:

> I like school but I get bored when I'm writing.

This was what one child reported when he'd finished his work:

> I like to finish early then I just get odd jobs to do while the others are finishing. Sometimes we're given another piece of work.

Also they felt that little time was given for them to think. They were reprimanded unless they were actively involved in writing:

Sometimes I get distracted, it happens quite a lot. If I say I'm thinking, it doesn't get believed. I'd like our teacher to give us more time to do our work. I don't like rushing things.

Repeated instruction from the teacher also led to the child becoming bored:

I think those who know should be allowed to get on with another piece of work and the teacher should teach those who don't know.

Cooperation between school and home

Achievers		
Parents	**Teachers**	**Children**
• Nine out of ten parents interviewed report good cooperation between parents and teacher • One thought child not worked hard enough • One embarrassed to talk of child's ability, apologetic	• Parents thought to be mainly supportive but two were over-anxious • Two parents are resented because they felt that their children should be challenged more • Nine children not handled well at home – have become arrogant • Expectations should not just be school created but must come from home as well	• All children are provided with topic books from home – supported in that way • All children talk of parents helping them with work at home if needed

Under-achievers		
Parents	**Teachers**	**Children**
• Some parents embarrassed when talking to teacher about child being able – feel teacher has to be approached in an apologetic manner • Ability not recognised by teacher • Not enough help or recognition given • School has got to respect parents' wishes	• In the main, the parents are supportive, although some are not aware of how they can help • A small percentage are not really interested – they don't value education • Some don't recognise child's ability • Too much pressure to achieve • Negative opinions about the school not being helpful	• Majority of children are sometimes provided with topic books from home, others receive no support at all • Majority talk of parents helping them with work at home

Some parents felt embarrassed and apologetic when approaching their child's teacher:

> I feel embarrassed talking about Harriet as an able child. It's almost as if you're apologising ... I always seem to be on the defensive.

One parent felt there was little cooperation between parents and teachers at her daughter's school. Although they had spoken to the teacher on a number of occasions, their daughter was not extended enough. Other parents, however, were very happy with the relationships they had formed with their child's teacher:

> It's important that a school teaches respect for others. I've been very happy with the school in all respects. [Parent governor]

Like the parents of achievers, parents of under-achievers reported that they felt embarrassed when talking to teachers about their son's or daughter's ability. The teacher had to be approached in an apologetic manner and they often felt that the child's ability was not recognised by him/her:

> On parents' evening I feel embarrassed. I go in an apologetic manner. No wonder the child wants to hide any ability. I think it's part of the British unwillingness to say, 'You're an achiever, go out there and achieve'.

Teachers thought that parents of achieving children were very supportive, although some were thought to be over-anxious. They thought parents were anxious that their children should be constantly challenged and were resented by some teachers because of this. The teachers felt that some children were not handled well at home and some of them consequently became arrogant.

In the main it was believed by teachers of under-achieving children that most parents were supportive, although some parents were not aware of how they could help. They also felt that some parents didn't value education while others didn't recognise a child's ability or didn't think it important. One parent in particular had been openly hostile and had repeated her negative opinions about the school to her child. It was generally felt that children needed to be aware that expectations were not just school-created but that they had to be supported at home. At the other extreme, there were parents who placed too much emphasis on their child achieving and this was counter-productive.

The achieving children all reported being supported in their work at home. The majority had help from parents with school work, if they needed it. Also a wide variety of books was available to them. The following quotation was typical of all three schools:

> If I really need help they will tell me how but they won't do it for me.

The following quotation is probably more typical of children from schools whose intake was not predominantly working class.

We have loads of books at home, the place is full of them – encyclopaedias, factual books, dictionaries, even cookery books in the kitchen.

Of the under-achieving children the majority talked about their parents supporting them at times with the provision of books to help with particular topics, but others received no help at all, or at least gave no indication that they felt that their parents had an interest in their schooling.

Emotional problems

Achievers		
Parents	**Teachers**	**Children**
• Harriet – night terrors; child regarded as an oddity – no friends • Bryony's brother's death has disturbed her	• Harriet seen as being full of herself • Bryony could be arrogant but her emotional problems were evident in her written work for a while	No comment

Under-achievers		
Parents	**Teachers**	**Children**
• Missed father – social repercussions – no friends • Inconsistent discipline from father • Too much pressure to achieve • Irritable – can't form relationships; manipulative, domineering • Very insecure • Mother admits to being over-protective	• Little comment apart from saying that home background affects their ability to achieve	Few comments were made • Two children miss their father

Evidence about emotional problems is coloured by a person's perspective and individuals are willing to share these perspectives only to varying degrees. Thus we have different stories and different amounts of information for each child. A flavour is provided here for readers to form their own opinions. Only two of the achievers had emotional problems, Harriet and Bryony. Harriet's mother had spoken of her 'night terrors' and her anxiety about feeling 'different' from everyone else. Her mother described this:

She's a poor sleeper, afraid of the dark and this has increased since she has grown older. She has vivid dreams. The latest things are out of body experiences. She has night terrors. It's not knowing where you are but waking up and finding you are nowhere, being detached, not feeling anything and everything is grey. It physically shakes her. She frightens herself. It was at the time when she was going through the bullying phase at school.

She went on to speak of Harriet's feelings of being 'different':

She sometimes feels she's an observer, looking down on what she's doing, rather than being there and feeling it. She has this fear that she doesn't fit in anywhere.

Harriet's problems clearly do have something to do with school and her relationships. Many able children do feel different but perhaps not to such an extent. Bryony, although very upset by her brother's death, seemed to have survived without it having affected her work negatively. Her mother remarked:

The death of her brother affected her badly. It brought the feeling of death closer to her.

However, such was the close nature of the two remaining children and the parents, who were all very supportive of each other, that Bryony seemed to take this unhappy incident in her stride.

With the under-achieving children, emotional problems seemed to be frequently associated with divorce. Edward, whose parents divorced when he was two years old, found it very difficult to socialise. His mother told of his early days at school:

He wouldn't speak at all at play school or nursery school. He sat with his back to the class. He never indulged in dramatic play and is still very withdrawn. He has no real friends.

Jane, another child, was very insecure. Her parents divorced when she was five years old. Her mother talked about the early part of her life:

Too much pressure was placed upon her to achieve early on by her father. His discipline was very inconsistent and consequently she's very insecure.

Another child, Sarah, was subjected to violence preceding divorce and this had resulted in the child becoming emotionally disturbed and displaying behaviour which was not conducive to achieving at school. She had poor skills of concentration and little motivation. In addition to this she seemed unable to make lasting relationships with anyone.

Yet another child who seemed to have suffered as a result of divorce was Alexander, who was rather withdrawn. The explanation for this, as far as his mother was concerned, was that Alexander was bullied by his sister who was two years older. Karl had divorced parents. He too was a shy child who was anxious to please but whose work proceeded at a very slow pace. His mother was unable to put forward an explanation for this other than saying that he was very meticulous.

As soon as his mother returned from work each day, he tried to impress her with what he had done:

> He does take a long time to do mundane things such as getting dressed. He's very meticulous ... He is constantly trying to show me how hard he tries and how good he is.

Alistair exhibited disturbed behaviour, not because of divorce, but because he had been over-protected, as his mother willingly confessed:

> Alistair was our second child. Our first died a cot death at two weeks old. He was born three years after that so we've paid an extreme amount of attention to him.

This led to his parents being over-anxious about his progress, as can be understood.

By her teacher Harriet was seen as being extremely confident. He described her as liking to 'pontificate' but he acknowledged that she had social problems. Although Bryony's teacher found her arrogant and insolent at times, she did not feel that the death of her brother had affected her too adversely, as she had obviously progressed. At the end of the year her teacher had this to say:

> She has developed well in all areas and has shown real commitment and effort.

There was a time when she would write rather mournful poems but that phase seemed to be over.

Of the children who were under-achieving and had emotional difficulties, teachers felt that the home background had a major part to play in this. This in turn was reflected in their work and their ability to socialise. The following summarises the teachers' viewpoints.

Alexander had a very domineering step-father. His mother had married for the third time and Alexander was the child of her first marriage. She worked full time and there was a constant stream of au pairs to look after the children. They didn't stay long because they did not find Alexander's step-father easy to work for. Alistair's teacher felt that, with his mother, his disruptive behaviour had been allowed to go unchecked. His teacher had witnessed this. He was very immature and inconsiderate of other children. His teacher remarked:

> He's so egocentric that he completely alienates other children.

However, she did feel that his mother's over-protection and negative attitude towards the school had affected him adversely. Karl seemed rather over-awed by his extremely confident mother. Although he seemed happy enough at home, his teacher wondered if his mother's expectations of him were too high. Sarah's teacher talked of the emotional battering which she had had and how this had affected both her work and social behaviour.

The children made few comments. Sarah said that she was unable to see her father now and Toby talked of never having experienced family life, because his father left when he was a baby. During observation sessions, children from single-parent families had been frequently overheard talking about not being able to afford things which other children had, something that was not observed for children from intact families. Perhaps this was their way of indicating that all was not right with their world.

Illustrations of results

Case records were compiled for all the children in this study. The primary consideration was that for each case being studied, the information was as complete as possible. This included all the interview material from parents, teachers and children; observation data; documentary evidence (children's narratives, children's records and portfolios); as well as statistical evidence gained from the quantitative aspect of the research.

Any redundant material was filtered out at this stage to provide a comprehensive and holistic picture in each case record. The cases were then compared and contrasted, highlighting recurrent themes and providing an opportunity to note what patterns of factors were common for achievers and under-achievers. It became clear through this process that no one factor alone could be isolated as a primary cause of under-achievement. Diagrams of achievers and under-achievers were devised, taking all the data into consideration (Figures 5.4 and 5.5).

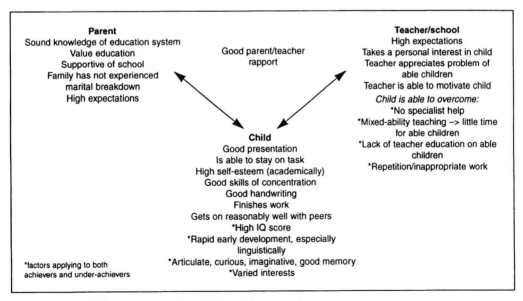

Figure 5.4   Diagram associated with achievement

A number of factors inter-relate, overlap and support each other to aid achievement, those particularly salient being supportive parents and teachers who act in cooperation while the child has good skills of concentration and presentation, task commitment, high self-esteem and ability to relate well to peers. Achievement is restricted when various combinations of some of these factors are missing.

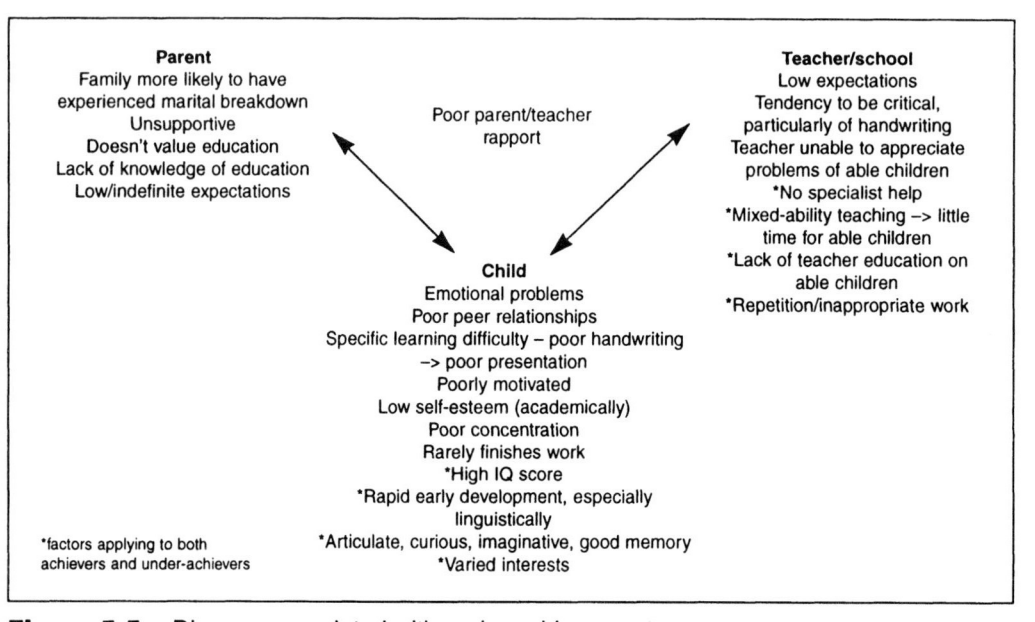

Figure 5.5   Diagram associated with under-achievement

Salient points connected with achievement and under-achievement

For the achieving child, each part of the diagram has equal importance, and the majority of achieving children fitted into this pattern. Consequently it is presented in its entirety as representative of the typical achieving able child and his/her environment.

The diagram for the under-achiever, however, is more complex. A child who experiences all of the problems illustrated in the diagram is certainly likely to under-achieve. Combinations of some of these factors may or may not result in under-achievement, depending on the particular child and other supportive aspects of his/her environment. Viewing all the factors associated with under-achievement in comparison with the children in this study, a histogram displaying the difficulties these children may experience and their predominance has been constructed (Figure 5.6).

The levels of predominance shown in Figure 5.6 are indicators of under-achievement and should alert both parents and teachers to the possibility of a child under-achieving. As may be seen from the histogram, factors which attain the first level of predominance, being applicable to 14 of the 16 under-achievers, are poor motivation, poor skills of concentration and rarely finishing tasks set. These appear

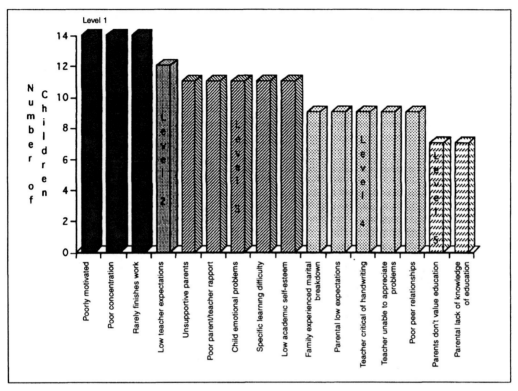

Figure 5.6   Levels of predominance of factors associated with under-achievement

to be connected and should be noted by parents and teachers as important indicators of under-achievement. It is possible however, that some of the factors, such as those in level one, especially motivation, may be the result of the influence of one or more of the other factors.

At the second level of predominance is low teacher expectations. Teachers should be wary of the effect that their attitudes can have on children. If children realise that teachers expect little of them, then many will do as little work as possible. It is conceivable that low teacher expectations contribute towards the factors described at the first level of predominance. Rosenthal and Jacobson (1968) found that children fulfilled and reacted to their teacher's expectations, and perhaps the same could be said of the children in this study.

This is possibly related to lack of teacher education regarding the able child. The ability of an under-achieving child is not always apparent. His/her written output may be minimal and there may be a large gap between oral and written work. The reasons for this may be emotional and hidden from the teacher. Possibly the child is working at a level that is on a par with that of the average child but he/she may have superior comprehension and retention of concepts when interested. Alternatively the child may be under-achieving because he/she doesn't want to appear different from his/her peers.

To avoid under-achieving children being overlooked, it is incumbent on the teacher to know and understand his/her pupils well. One of the attributes of good teaching most commonly adduced by children was that a teacher should take a personal interest in each pupil. It is realised that teachers have heavy workloads, but greater personal knowledge of their children could yield positive results in a number of ways. Some of these are: creating a better rapport with the child; having a clearer knowledge of assignments which motivate a child; having a deeper understanding of the difficulties experienced by the under-achieving child. Attending to some of these might even make the task of the class teacher easier.

At the third level of predominance is unsupportive parents, poor parent/teacher rapport, emotional problems, a specific learning difficulty (notably handwriting) and low academic self-esteem. A notable element associated with under-achievement is lack of parental support and the reasons for this may be varied. Time constraints/emotional stress which marital breakdown places on a single parent may affect a child negatively. Conversely parents may be unsupportive in that they put too much pressure on the child to achieve. All this can influence parent/teacher rapport and, if communication between a school and a parent is poor, then it is possible that the child will suffer.

The other factors which influence under-achievement at this level are centred around the children. Emotional disturbance can affect a child in a number of ways and can lead to under-achievement. A specific learning difficulty may be concealed by an able child because in other respects he/she is working at a level which is on a par with the average child. It is a pity that as a result of a specific learning difficulty not being recognised in an able child, potential may be lost and this may have life-long repercussions.

Low academic self-esteem also seems influential when considering under-achievement. Eleven out the 16 under-achievers appeared to have a low academic self-esteem. This result was arrived at through collating interview and observation data rather than just using the child's self-rating. As the research progressed, the researcher got to know the children on a personal basis and was better able to make 'personal judgements'. This is at variance with the result attained by the test of self-esteem as detailed in the first part of this chapter, but is possibly more accurate. During the test, the children were possibly trying to present a good impression, particularly academically, whereas during observation sessions they were busy and likely to have forgotten that they were being observed, as the observer was accepted as a teacher/helper in the classroom.

Patton (1990) was of the opinion that covert observations were more likely to capture what was really happening than overt observations when the people in the setting were acutely aware that they were being studied. This is a possible explanation for the discrepancy. In the literature, low self-esteem is associated with under-achievement as reported by Fine and Pitts (1980), Whitmore (1980, 1986,

1988), Covington (1984) and Gleason (1988), and is supported by this study if the researcher's estimation is accepted.

All these problems for able children who fail to achieve are exacerbated by the following:

- non-existent or insufficient specialist help within the school;
- mixed-ability teaching, where the teacher is so occupied with the needs of the less able and average children that little time is left for the able child;
- lack of teacher education on the able child;
- children being made to repeat work, or to do repetitious or inappropriate work.

The fact that there has been little teacher education on able children in the past has possibly led to a lack of understanding of the plight of the able child on the part of the teacher. This accounts in part for the inappropriate work which many of the children in this study were set. In addition, large classes of children of mixed ability, where there is little or no specialist help, do little to alleviate the pressures which teachers are under and do nothing to help the under-achiever.

Conclusion

This chapter has drawn together the threads which were unravelled during the interviews. Opinions, observations and insights from parents, teachers, children and from the researcher herself, in addition to the quantitative data, have been brought together to construct the diagrams of an achieving and an under-achieving child.

The factors contained in each of the diagrams, both those intrinsic and extrinsic to the child, interact in various ways, combinations of factors being apparently more significant than the presence or absence of single factors.

Chapter 6

Case Studies of Achieving Able Children

In the previous chapter we have identified some of the factors related to achievement and under-achievement. How some of these are lived out in real life is illustrated by case studies in this and the following chapter. In this chapter, two children will be considered: Harriet, aged 11, and Jack, aged 10, both achieving able children. Harriet was in Year 6 and Jack in Year 5 and they attended different schools. Both will be discussed from a number of perspectives: those of the parent, teacher, child and the researcher. The length of each report varies as some people are naturally less forthcoming than others.

Information derived from repertory grids completed both by children and by teachers is included here. These grids give the reader an understanding of the way the child or teacher makes sense of an aspect of his/her world and those attributes which are most important to that person. A fuller explanation of the method of construction appears later in the chapter, and Chapter 9 will explore how the approach underpinning this exploratory tool can be used to good effect by teachers.

Extracts from children's work appear in the text exactly as they were written.

Harriet

Sketch of the child

Harriet was an extremely attractive child. She was tall and slim with blue eyes and blonde hair. She was endowed with a quiet confidence and was always willing to talk to me whenever she was visited. Her mother was a teacher and Harriet's father had his own computer consultancy business. She had an older brother and a sister. Although she was an achiever, she did have social difficulties. Although there were a number of able children in the same class as Harriet and many of these had found compatibility with each other, Harriet was not one of these.

The parents' perspective

Mrs Terry, Harriet's mother, put some of Harriet's difficulties down to the fact that her teachers did not know how to deal with her:

> As a teacher I know that there are very few training courses devoted to able children.

Mrs Terry went on to say that Harriet had a poor opinion of herself socially. This stemmed from the fact that she was seen as being different by her peers. She often asked her mother why she had to try so hard for people to like her. Mrs Terry commented:

> It's a very difficult gift to deal with, it's the way she thinks. What she says can sound challenging. She isn't intimidated by people in authority. She has to dominate in any class discussion. This often gets a negative feedback from peers and teachers.

Harriet was often rejected by her peers, 'put in her place' by teachers and, as a result, she felt that she didn't fit in anywhere. This feeling was even extended to her own family, which greatly worried her parents. Harriet was their third child. Both her brother and sister were able but were not as able as Harriet. They did not have Harriet's social problems and because of that did not envy her at all.

Harriet had recently gone through a phase of depression. This had resulted in her not eating or sleeping. At Christmas she sent cards to herself addressed 'To the ugly one', 'To the fat one', which her parents were understandably distressed about.

The family doctor attributed this depression to not being adequately provided for at school and referred her to an educational psychologist. The psychologist said that he was unable to deal with her problems and suggested that an advisory teacher for the gifted visit the school. After three sessions with Harriet, she was unable to visit the school any more as she was so much in demand throughout the county. However, although she acted in an advisory capacity to the school, the work set for Harriet did not seem to change.

Despite being labelled by her school as a highly able child, no individual programme of study was specially designed for her. She did the same work as others in her group and often had to do repeat exercises, supposedly for consolidation purposes – for example particular mathematical processes – which she had readily grasped. Often she was told to do another page of the same sort of work if she finished before other members of the class.

As quoted in the previous chapter, Mrs Terry often felt that she had to approach teachers in an apologetic way when talking about Harriet. Her final comment was as follows:

> I think it's hard to have an able child in the state system. Sometimes I wish she wasn't gifted because life would be so much easier. I think she would be a happier person. It's a shame because it should be a positive thing.

The teacher's perspective

Both Harriet and Fergus (see the following chapter for case notes on Fergus) were in the same class. In this class pupils were expected to sit in one seat for a particular activity and to work quietly. However, they were allowed a certain degree of movement. Talk between pupils was tolerated but this was rarely enough to distract others from working. The teacher was always in control; generally there were few disciplinary problems in the school. The percentage of pupils statemented for behavioural difficulties in the academic year 1993–4 was 1 per cent. Classroom rules, although determined by the teacher, were kept. Sanctions included working through playtimes and ultimately being sent to the headteacher.

Group work was practised but pupils tended to work at the same subject at the same time. They sat in groups with pupils of like ability. Topics tended to be inter-disciplinary. Homework was given but was usually something which had to be finished rather than a specific task. This school was neither wholly formal nor wholly informal, but a mixture of the two.

During his interview, Mr Perrott, Harriet's teacher, showed an awareness of her social difficulties and appreciated how different she was from the majority of other children in the class:

> She has a remarkable vocabulary and talks on a different intellectual plane. They think she's superior because she likes to discuss – pontificate would be a better word – at an advanced level. She can be very outspoken. Also she's quite manipulative. During group work she is often dogmatic and argumentative. She is not well organised.

All her written work was considered to be good, her powers of concentration excellent and she was able to work independently. He thought her self-esteem, with regard to academic work, was high. In his opinion, she was not good at games.

In Mr Perrott's consideration, Harriet was not isolated academically because there were other clever children in the class. He was fully aware that children such as Harriet needed stimulation and expressed the opinion that in such cases tasks set by the teacher should be challenging.

Harriet's story

Harriet began her 'memoirs', as she called them, by stating her belief that she was born under an unlucky star. She elaborated on this by saying that she had read that on the day she was born a chunk of plaster fell from the ceiling in the Parthenon in Athens and it was consequently closed.

She recalled starting her education by being thought of as a problem child by both teachers and parents. She was determined to do just as she wanted but acknowledged that she sometimes caused distress:

My parents thought that I was going to be a difficult child at school. So I was ... but in a different way.

Harriet didn't expand on her difficulties too much but implied that these revolved around teachers being unable to occupy her. She talked about her feelings on leaving her first school:

When I left Elmridge all my friends came with me. I had quite a lot of friends but I did not have a best friend. This is because I felt different from everyone. I wanted a friend who was just the same as me. I haven't found anyone like me yet but I'm still looking.

Later on in her narrative, she volunteered more about her social unease as she reached Year 5:

At the beginning of the year I found it more and more difficult to relate to my friends. I was different to them and they didn't like it. My friends seemed immature and younger than me, even though they were the same age. The things they liked to do seemed pointless and vice-versa. They used to call me 'brainbox', 'swot', 'clever clogs' and other names. I don't think they meant to be malicious but they hurt me and made me more self-dependent, liking solitude.

She recalled how quickly she learnt different tasks at her first school and how she was teased because she was constantly reading:

The teachers would tease me about having to step over me in the corridor while I was reading. There was a series of books which I loved. They were about flying horses and carved animals that came alive and I believe that they encouraged me to use my imagination more and more. Imagination, I think is a vital part of life.

Her comments about her teachers were few. In Year 5 she had a sympathetic teacher and she liked her very much. In her last year at primary school however, she and her teacher were often at odds. His comments on her lack of prowess on the games field really upset her:

I get very upset sometimes, for instance when my teacher has told me that I am less graceful than a squashed lump on the road, or that I run like a duck.

Consequently, she lost confidence completely during games and PE lessons. At the end of her last year in primary school her parents decided to send her to an independent school. Her 'memoirs' end on a very positive note, with the prospect of a new start at a single-sex convent school:

The memory I think that stands out is January 7th, the day of my entrance exam. It was snowy and cold that day and we had to drive to Bramley Convent where I was put in room 9. I knew no one else there and I was indescribably nervous. This exam was to decide my future. The exams weren't really hard. I had two maths, two English and one verbal reasoning. I was unable to tell anyone whether it had gone well or not. A couple of weeks later, my parents said they wanted to talk to me. They showed me a letter telling me that they were offering me a place at Bramley Convent. I was so happy. It was impossible to describe.

The researcher's perspective

After the first interview with Harriet, I was struck by the depth of her thinking and perception. Harriet was constantly reading and really enjoyed discussing her knowledge with people who were prepared to accept her. However, perhaps the most impressive thing about Harriet was her ability to write, which was exceptional. Harriet used her imagination to great effect in her writing. Figure 6.1 shows the opening part of a story entitled 'Revenge'.

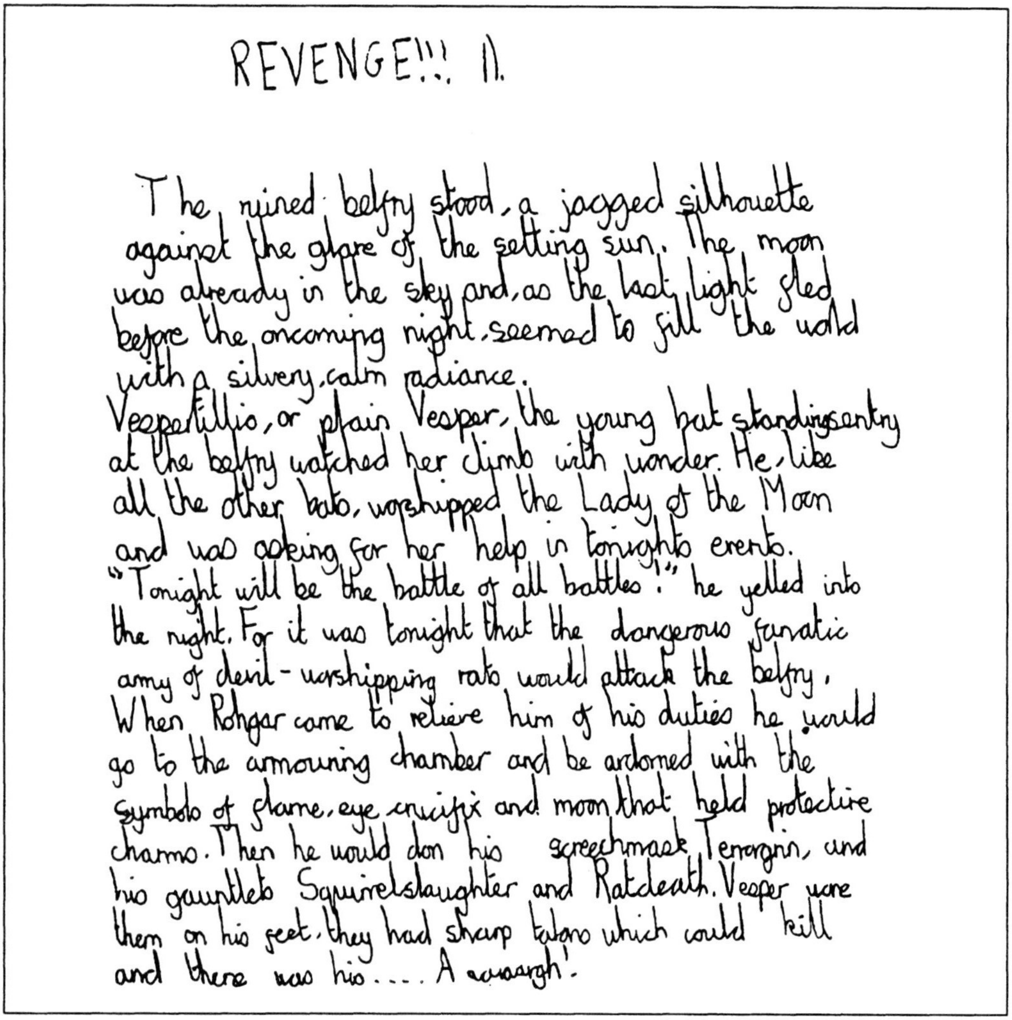
REVENGE!!! 1).

The ruined belfry stood, a jagged silhouette against the glare of the setting sun. The moon was already in the sky and, as the last light fled before the oncoming night, seemed to fill the world with a silvery, calm radiance.
Vespertillio, or plain Vesper, the young bat standing sentry at the belfry watched her climb with wonder. He, like all the other bats, worshipped the Lady of the Moon and was asking for her help in tonights events.
"Tonight will be the battle of all battles!" he yelled into the night. For it was tonight that the dangerous fanatic army of devil-worshipping rats would attack the belfry. When Rohgar came to relieve him of his duties he would go to the armouring chamber and be adorned with the symbols of flame, eye, crucifix and moon that held protective charms. Then he would don his screechmask Terragrin, and his gauntlets Squirrelslaughter and Ratdeath. Vesper wore them on his feet, they had sharp talons which could kill and there was his.... Aaaaargh'.

Figure 6.1 Harriet's work

These abilities set her apart from many others and caused difficulties with peers. They saw her as being odd and this made friendships difficult. Although Harriet did mention her social isolation, the degree of unhappiness which her mother mentioned was not recounted. Observation of lessons and periods in the playground, however, made this apparent. She was always alone. Her parents clearly found this aspect very difficult to handle.

From the observation of class lessons, Harriet's questions were not always well received. In fact on a couple of occasions her teacher became quite annoyed with her, possibly because her questions seemed a little obscure. He might instead have made use of these questions by turning them into opportunities for her to do her own research. Harriet noticed her teacher's attitude, because she had reported to her mother that she was often 'cut short' or 'fobbed off'.

Although her teacher appreciated that Harriet was an extremely able child, the impression given was that he resented her constant questioning. He talked of her 'pontificating', an unusual word to use with reference to a child. The children in his class always appeared busy, but the work set for the children included in this study was not always appropriate. When tasks were completed, the children were asked to do a similar task, to read or to illustrate topic work. It seemed particularly wasteful for a child to sit colouring the borders of topic pages during prime learning time.

Repertory grids

Repertory grids were used to glean information about the way in which both teacher and child viewed each other. The teachers were asked to select six able children from their class and these formed the elements for their repertory grids. They then compared them in threes to ascertain what was similar about two and different about the third. In this way they were able to identify constructs – for example two children might have good handwriting while the third might have difficulties in this respect. They would then ascribe a number to the child which would represent the child's place on the continuum 'good handwriting >>>> poor handwriting'.

The children were asked to select teachers who had taught them and these became their elements. They then compared them in a manner similar to that undertaken by the teachers. The teacher and pupil profiles which appear below were taken from repertory grids and present in graphical terms the views which children and teachers had of each other. The constructs which each one chose to include in their repertory grid, and the values they attached to each construct, illustrate the important points on a scale of 1–5.

Harriet's view of Mr Perrott

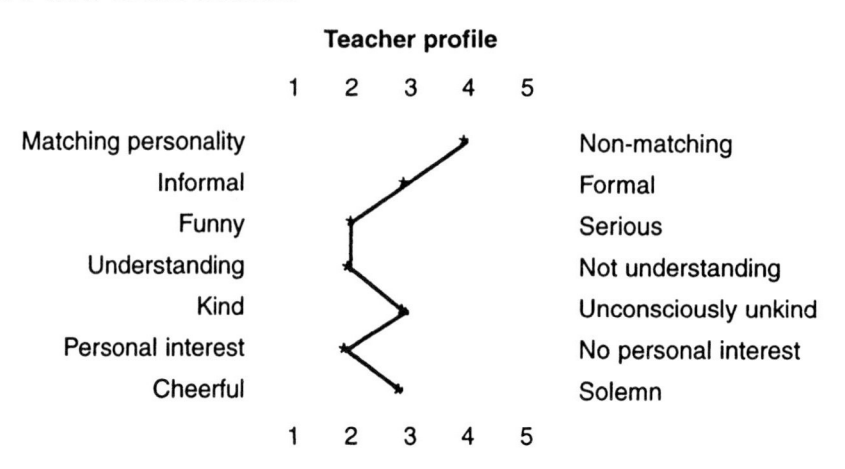

Harriet saw kindness, understanding, taking a personal interest in her, being funny, informal, having a personality which matched hers and being cheerful, as desirable attributes to have in a teacher. 'Having a matching personality' is quite a sophisticated concept for a child of this age. Although she didn't rate him as highly as her last teacher, she saw Mr Perrott as being fairly understanding, taking a personal interest in her and as being quite funny. He was reasonably kind, informal and cheerful but his personality certainly didn't match hers.

Mr Perrott's view of Harriet

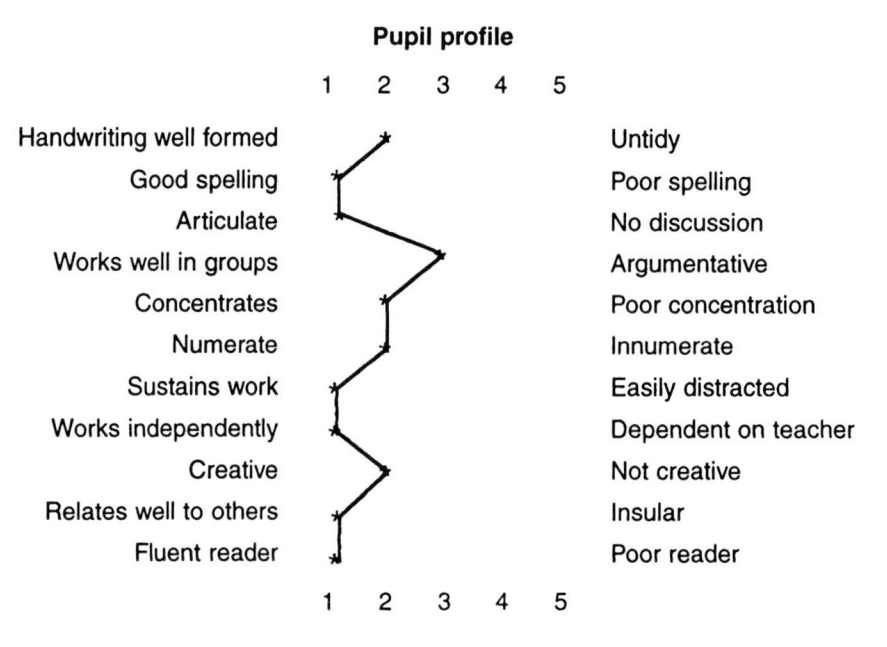

Mr Perrott felt that well-formed writing, good spelling, being articulate, having an ability to share work within a group, concentration, mental numeracy, the ability to sustain work, to be able to work independently, creativity, relating well to peers and adults and reading with fluency and understanding to be important factors with regard to children's achievement. Harriet's spelling, her ability to articulate, to sustain work, to work independently, to be creative, to relate well to peers and adults and to read with fluency and understanding, were all very good. Numeracy, handwriting, concentration and creativity were good but her ability to share or work in a group was only reasonable, in his view.

Researcher's comment

It was surprising, knowing the social difficulties which Harriet experienced, that Mr Perrott saw her ability to relate well to peers and adults as being good. Verbal clashes between Mr Perrott and Harriet had been witnessed in the classroom and Harriet's isolation outside the classroom was only too apparent. The fact that he rated her ability to share or to work in a group as only reasonable seemed at variance with his earlier verbal evaluation. This second evaluation would seem to be a more realistic assessment.

Harriet's assessment of Mr Perrott seemed to be neither wholly positive nor wholly negative. Rather, it struck a middle chord. Generally Mr Perrott's assessment of Harriet was positive, although he clearly found her hard to deal with as a pupil.

Jack

Sketch of the child

Jack was tall and slim with an athletic figure. He had light brown hair and blue eyes. Academically he was very competent and he was equally so on the sports field. He had a brother who was two years younger. His father was a sergeant in the army and his mother worked part-time in a shop but was always at home when the children finished school. The children were firmly disciplined. At the same time, both Mr and Mrs Sullivan seemed caring parents and both boys appeared very happy.

The parents' perspective

Both parents were interviewed.

Jack's early physical and mental progress was fast. Mrs Sullivan spent a great deal of time playing with him when he was very young and was particularly impressed with his language development. She had always found his constant questioning wearing and still did, but tried to answer him to the best of her ability. He started to read at three and a half years. He had always been eager to learn and they had done their best to help him.

Both parents gave the impression that they wanted Jack to have a good education and to go on to university. They wanted him to have the opportunity that they had not had; neither went on to higher education. At the same time Mr Sullivan would have liked him to become a professional footballer. The house was full of the cups Jack had won for sport and it seemed as though he could probably do this, if he so desired. His other interests included athletics and boxing, and he had an insatiable appetite for reading.

They thought him very mature for his age and he was independent. He liked to make sure that his sports kit and school books were packed ready for school and did not rely on his mother to do this. At times they felt he needed to be by himself, away from the family, and he was left to his own devices on those occasions.

Jack's concentration and attention span were good and he spent hours in his bedroom if there was work to be done. He was also a perfectionist and would repeat an assignment if a mistake had been made. His written English displayed imagination and he had an extremely good memory. He was able to remember details of incidents which happened years ago. However, he was temperamental and got upset if he was criticised.

Socially, he never had any problems. Although seen as a leader among his peers, he didn't resort to bullying. Other adults had often complimented Mr and Mrs Sullivan on his behaviour. Mr and Mrs Sullivan felt that Jack was a confident boy and that his self-esteem was high. They had only praise for the school and thought both his class and headteacher were excellent.

The teacher's perspective

The general ambience in this classroom was informal. Both Jack and Sarah (see case notes on Sarah in the next chapter) were in the same class. Classroom management was such that freedom of movement and talking were tolerated. Children often sat in different places, according to the task and groups in which they were working. They were grouped for ability for English and mathematics.

There were more disciplinary problems at this school than in the other two schools included in the study. The percentage of children statemented for behavioural difficulties in the academic year 1993–4 was 10 per cent. Classroom rules were determined by the teacher and the children together. There was a highly structured disciplinary procedure in place whereby three verbal warnings from the teacher, for breaches of classroom rules, resulted in withdrawal of privileges and extra work which was completed in the child's own time. Persistent disobedience occasioned a letter to the parents.

A variety of instructional strategies was used but emphasis was placed upon discovery-based learning with the teacher taking more of a consultative, guiding and stimulating role, rather than a didactic one. Group work took up the majority of the day (up to 75 per cent) with children working at different tasks and subjects. The groups were of mixed ability apart from those for English and mathematics. Free communication was allowed, with the teacher remaining in control but staying in the background.

A great deal of emphasis was placed upon topic work which was multi-disciplinary. Also presentation and art work were thought to be very important and this was extended to wall displays, which were extremely impressive. Mrs Jones thought Jack was conscientious and hard-working. He settled well to tasks and was able to persevere with new and unknown activities. He was popular but at times could be intolerant of those who were less able. He tended to dominate group discussions. However, he was reliable and was always polite to adults.

Written work was well organised and he produced interesting pieces of descriptive writing. He was able to apply his mathematical knowledge to problem solving and had made excellent progress. He enjoyed scientific investigation and was keen to develop his own follow-up tasks. He worked sensibly, with initiative. Generally, he enjoyed pursuing his own scientific thoughts. His investigations were always well planned and predictions were well thought out. All work was thoroughly recorded.

Jack was well coordinated and an outstanding athlete. He had a well developed sense of competition but he needed to keep a check on his team spirit. He sometimes needed to realise that not everyone was quite the sports person that he was.

Mrs Jones thought Jack had a high self-esteem and that his parents were very supportive. She thought it important for parents to have a sound knowledge of the education system. She commented:

> One of the biggest problems we seem to have here is that parents trust us. They don't challenge us at all. That's not healthy.

She thought that Jack would succeed because he not only had the intelligence to do so, but because he knew how to treat people socially. She described him as a mainstream achiever. In her opinion, he would not go into any sort of profession which included risk, but he would be successful nevertheless.

Jack's story

Jack thought he was good at most things in school. One thing he did not particularly like was listening to stories. He would rather read himself or do something practical. He said that his main interest was football, although he did like other sports. He was polite but self-contained in interviews.

The researcher's perspective

Jack was well motivated and worked hard in school. He was popular with his peers and his prowess on the sports field increased this. He was usually polite to adults but at times he could appear to be very arrogant. His parents seemed supportive of both Jack and the school and had no criticism to make of the school. Perhaps Mrs Jones was right in saying that parents were reluctant to challenge teachers at this school because they seemed to accept that teachers always knew best.

Figure 6.2 is an example of his written English, taken from a descriptive piece of prose. The task was to describe a storm as seen from an open window. It is well written and presented.

As I looked through the rain soaked window of our cosy Cornish holiday cottage, I sat and watched as the sky grew darker and darker. Other families scuttled about, unprepared for the sudden down-pour. As the barn door battered vigorously in the wind, it revealed two scruffy farm cats. All the birds fell silent or their songs were drowned out by the horrific sound of the storm. The patient cows gathered under the umbrella of the large oak trees either side of the entrance to their water logged field. Sheep and their nervous lambs were restless and bleated noisily at one another constantly trying to keep alongside their mums for comfort. The high Cornish hedges which earlier had looked light and colourful with delicate wild flowers and butterflies, were now bent double with the pain of the storm.

Figure 6.2 Jack's work

Repertory grids

As we saw earlier in the chapter, an exploration of the constructs of both teacher and child can be extremely illuminating.

Jack's view of Mrs Jones

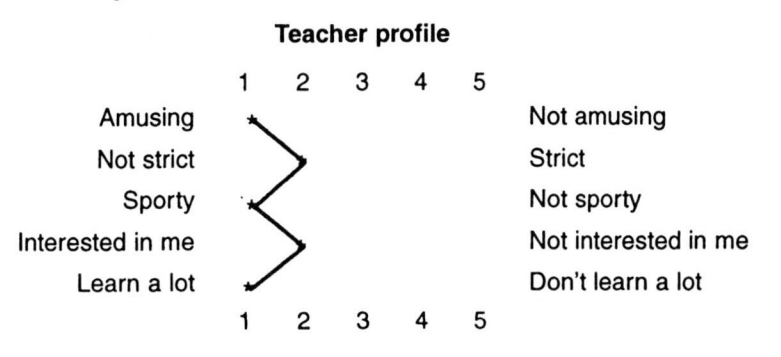

Jack thought the following attributes important for the ideal teacher: they should not be strict, but should be interested in him and should be sporty. In addition, they should be amusing and a pupil should learn a lot in their class. He thought very positively of Mrs Jones. He saw her as being not very strict and quite interested in him. She was very sporty, very amusing and he learnt a lot in her class.

Mrs Jones's view of Jack

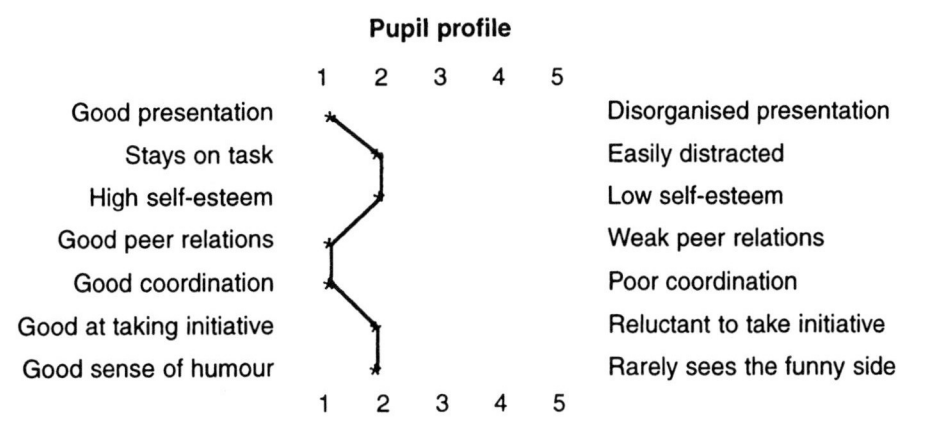

Mrs Jones saw the following constructs as being conducive to achievement: good coordination, good peer relations, the ability to stay on task, good presentation, high self-esteem, the ability to take initiative, having a good sense of humour.

In Jack she saw very good coordination, peer relationships, being able to stay on task and presentation skills. He had a high self-esteem, was good at taking initiative and had a good sense of humour.

Researcher's comment

Both Jack and Mrs Jones thought positively of each other and this was noticeable during observation sessions. Mrs Jones appeared to think of Jack as being a responsible person and he clearly enjoyed and was responsive to her praise.

A comparison of the two achieving able children

Although both Harriet and Jack are achievers, their portraits are very different. Harriet is achieving academically but has great difficulties socially. Jack, on the other hand, seems to achieve in all spheres. However, Harriet has the benefit of parents who are familiar with the education system and can help her academically. Jack's parents are supportive of the education system but have little experience of its higher levels from which to provide academic support. They may need to take advice from teachers later in Jack's school career, and so effective parent/teacher liaison will be extremely important.

This highlights the fact that not all apparently achieving children fit the mould of the happy, fulfilled child who is popular and has everything going for him/her. There may be problems beneath the surface and it is part of the job of teachers to identify these problems. For example, helping children to socialise is important and is something which can be assisted by parent/teacher liaison. This is discussed further in Chapter 10.

Chapter 7

Case Studies of Under-achieving Able Children

This chapter looks at three under-achieving able children, Fergus, aged 11, Sarah, aged 10 and Alistair, aged 11. Fergus and Alistair were in Year 6 and Sarah in Year 5. As in the last chapter, they will be viewed from a number of perspectives and repertory grids from the pupils and teachers will be included.

Fergus

Sketch of the child

Fergus was a tall, slim and rather ungainly boy with light brown hair. He talked readily to adults and seemed interested in a great many subjects. He was confident and seemed to enjoy life. Both of his parents were teachers, his father being a headteacher. He had an older brother whose intellectual ability was similar to Fergus's but who was achieving at school. According to Fergus's mother, they got on well together.

The parents' perspective

Fergus's mother, Mrs Jardine, was interviewed.

Fergus is reported as having developed rapidly both physically and mentally. He was stringing words together to make sentences before the age of two. Pre-school, Mrs Jardine did a lot of language work with him and, like Jack's mother, was astounded at how quickly his command of language grew. This was reflected in his spoken language but not in his written work. She said that in a discussion or argument, he would always win because of his reasoning powers. He was able to absorb information and retain it. When he was three he used with ease a computer program designed for infants.

However, his ability was rarely displayed in school work. This was a great cause for concern for his parents. His mother said he was not sufficiently motivated to do well at school. He found it difficult to practise things. If he could not succeed at once, he gave up. His lack of coordination was manifested in poor handwriting. In the past he had been told that his work was messy and untidy and he had to repeat it on numerous occasions. The effect of this was that Fergus thoroughly disliked writing. He was seen by an occupational therapist who suggested that he use a lap-top word processor. Mrs Jardine was reluctant for this to happen as she saw this as being defeatist.

His lack of coordination made him a poor sportsman and he felt badly about this. He enjoyed the social element of school so much and would have relished being a member of the football team. However, he enjoyed supporting his friends and went along to all the football matches. By doing this, he felt accepted as a member of the group:

> He feels it very much that he's not a footballer and all his friends are. We go and support the team and he stays and watches after school.

Another reason for under-achievement, which Mrs Jardine pointed to, was the fact that Fergus didn't like to appear different from his peers:

> It's my opinion that he'll under-achieve at school in order not to appear a boffin.

This opinion was supported by the following report. Fergus mentioned this to her after a discussion in school:

> He said that he had a really good discussion with Harriet. Then he said 'She's daft because she'll say it in class [express her views]. She finds it difficult to make friends because of it. The others think she's odd. She should shut up.'

Mrs Jardine had definite views about mixed-ability teaching:

> From the teacher's point of view it's very difficult to cater for the very able in a mixed-ability class. I do this myself. I often feel I am failing the able child in favour of the less able because they are so demanding. I feel that Fergus's under-achievement is a bit of Fergus and a bit of the teacher not being able to cope.

Mrs Jardine felt that although Fergus understood his work and could complete it quickly, he wouldn't tell his teacher he'd finished because then he'd be asked to do more of the same.

One area in which he really excelled was drama. Although motivated by very little else, he learned a script quickly. He was a member of a youth drama group and delighted in taking part. In fact this was the only activity he was really personally interested in. All other interests were superficial. This possibly stemmed from his reluctance to practise; his parents had tried to interest him in a number of activities but had failed. Mrs Jardine was concerned about his future:

> I'm hoping that eventually he'll discover what he wants to do in life and this will motivate his academic work.

There was another side of Fergus, however, that has not been discussed. Socially he was outstanding. He was extremely popular with his peers and also knew the best way to approach and to get on with adults. He had a strong sense of justice and represented his peers before adults if he thought there was a problem which ought to be settled.

Mrs Jardine felt that much more should be done for able children in schools:

> I'd like more opportunity for able children to work together. I'd like them to have special needs help on a regular basis, difficult and extending work.

Like Harriet's mother, she also felt that she had to approach the school in an apologetic manner when talking about Fergus:

> I don't believe there's enough being done for able children. On parents' evening I feel embarrassed. I go in an apologetic manner. I feel I should only talk about his social skills because if I talk about academic ability, it only looks as though I'm bragging. It's very difficult. No wonder the child wants to hide any ability. I feel it's part of our upbringing, our British unwillingness to say 'You're an achiever, go out there and achieve'.

Her final comment, if generally the case in primary schools, pointed to a great waste of potential:

> It's the gifted who are always left out and they're the leaders, the decision -makers of the future, the ones who should guide.

The teacher's perspective

Fergus's teacher thought that Fergus related well to peers and adults alike. He worked well in a group and was highly articulate. He was outstandingly good at drama. He read fluently but his handwriting was very poor and his concentration span not very long. He commented:

> One must be careful with a bright child because if they're not stretched, they can easily switch off. It's important that clever children don't feel excluded or different in any way.

Fergus's story

Fergus's first remark left one in no doubt as to what he valued most about school, namely the social aspect:

> My time at School B has been very successful. I've learnt to mix with all different sorts of children.

He said his strengths were maths and computer work. He also enjoyed science because he liked testing and experimenting but he enjoyed acting better than anything else. His weakness was English because he was not particularly good at handwriting:

> I find English a bit of a bore because I usually have to do it again.

He admitted to being accident prone. Examples of this are rolling 30 feet down a mountain and being saved by his rucksack, falling off his chair in school and having stitches in his head, and having numerous accidents on his bike. This was possibly connected with his lack of coordination, though he seemed to take his mishaps in his stride:

Apart from drama, he liked finding out about new inventions and looking at modern art. He tried to become interested in a number of activities but just did not have enough patience to persevere. He obviously wanted to be an expert straight away.

> I've tried numerous sporting activities. I remember when I did Judo for the first time, I got knocked out, literally, and had to go to hospital. I decided not to go again. I've tried short tennis, football, rugby, the piano, cornet, tenor horn but I haven't found anything which interests me yet, apart from drama.

The researcher's perspective

From personal observation it appeared that the able children in Fergus's class were often left to work unaided. However, as his teacher rightly pointed out, able children have to be constantly challenged or stretched if they are to maintain their motivation. This could be one of the reasons why Fergus was interested in so little at school. Fergus's mother made reference to the difficulties in mixed-ability teaching and this was certainly a point worthy of consideration.

Fergus's handwriting was poor, but repetition only seemed to make the matter worse. The child had come to dislike English because of this. With specialist support this situation could possibly have been avoided. Fergus was eager not to appear different from his peers and hid his ability to gain acceptance. In his reported discussion with Harriet he showed a maturity beyond his years.

Mrs Jardine's reluctance and embarrassment which she felt when talking to Fergus's teacher about her son's academic ability displayed a lack of conveyed understanding on the part of the teacher and a breakdown in parent/teacher communication. The account of the Sutton Hoo Burial in Figure 7.1 is an example of Fergus's written English, taken from his portfolio. As can be seen, he did have problems, although the presentation here is his best and much better than in his books.

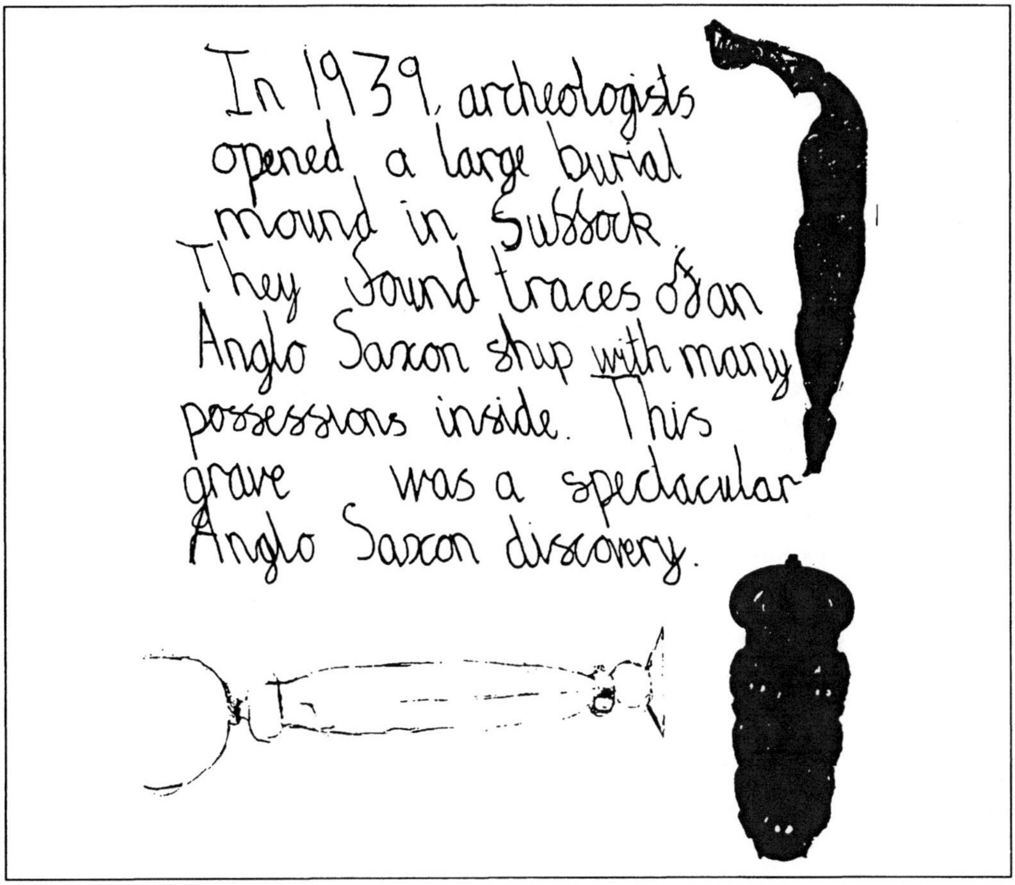

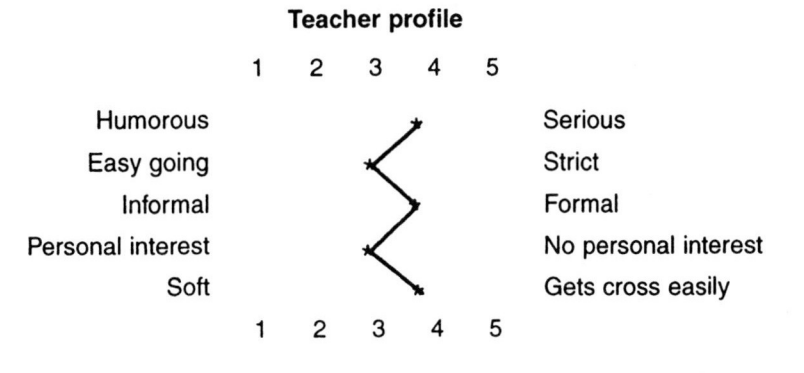

Figure 7.1 Fergus's work

Repertory grids

Fergus's view of Mr Perrott

Teacher profile

	1	2	3	4	5	
Humorous				×		Serious
Easy going		×				Strict
Informal				×		Formal
Personal interest		×				No personal interest
Soft				×		Gets cross easily

1 2 3 4 5

From Fergus's point of view, an ideal teacher should be easy going, take a personal interest in him, be humorous, be soft as opposed to getting cross easily, and should teach informally. Mr Perrott was perceived as being fairly easy going and taking a reasonable personal interest in him but he was also serious, a teacher who got cross easily and whose teaching was formal.

Mr Perrott's view of Fergus

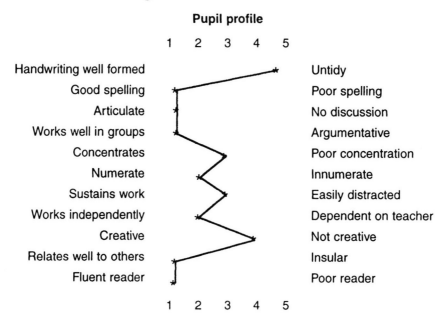

Pupil profile

Mr Perrott felt that well-formed writing, good spelling, being articulate, having an ability to share work within a group, concentration, mental numeracy, the ability to sustain work, to be able to work independently, creativity, relating well to peers and adults and reading with fluency and understanding to be important factors with regard to children's achievement.

He saw Fergus as being very good at the following: spelling, sharing and working in a group and relating to peers and adults. He was perceived as being highly articulate and as reading fluently. Also he was capable of working independently and was numerate. However, his ability to concentrate and to sustain work was not particularly good. His handwriting was also regarded as being very poor and he was not felt to be very creative, although it may be that the latter is masked by the former.

Researcher's comment

Fergus's assessment of Mr Perrott was slightly negative whereas Mr Perrott's assessment of Fergus struck a middle ground, although he did score highly for five attributes. During observation sessions, interaction between the two seemed amicable but it was noticeable that Mr Perrott became rather irritated by Fergus's lack of concentration.

Sarah

Outline of the child

Sarah was tall and slim with short blonde hair. She came from a family which had experienced marital breakdown. Her father was violent and both she and her brother lived with her mother. Her father was a corporal in the army and her mother a nurse.

The parents' perspective

Sarah's mother (Mrs Grant) was interviewed.

Sarah's early development, i.e. speech and coordination, was reported as rapid. She read at three years and was reading newspapers pre-school. She was always an inquisitive child and this had continued; she was constantly questioning. Her vocabulary was very good but she disliked writing and would do anything to avoid it. She was only self-disciplined if the subject aroused her interest. She liked to organise others, for example during group activities, but failed to organise herself.

She had a fairly wide range of interests. She was an avid reader, enjoyed history and current affairs. She would play an active part during discussions with obvious enjoyment. As far as her attitude to school was concerned, she did not totally dislike it. As her mother remarked:

> She enjoys learning but doesn't like fitting in.

Her mother thought she was very arrogant and tended to talk down to people. She thought Sarah's self-esteem was high. With regard to expectations, Mrs Grant seemed to have no particular ambition for her daughter:

> Sarah will achieve because she is ruthless, reckless and determined but she wouldn't have the patience to go to a university because she has no sticking power.

Mrs Grant did not seem to value education and thought that Sarah would achieve without it. Her comment when asked about higher education was:

> I'm not interested in knowledge.

Sarah was apparently very irritable at home. Her temper tantrums wore Mrs Grant out, as her comment implies:

> She doesn't have a lot of time for others. She's manipulative and domineering. She uses people but doesn't give in return. She's been demanding from birth.

Apparently there was a constant power struggle between mother and daughter. Mrs Grant wanted respect but got none from Sarah. She was often rude to her mother. She treated her brother badly – for example verbally abusing or ignoring him.

Mrs Grant thought Sarah was very materialistic, wanting to live in a better house, having possessions similar to those of other children. She was aware, however, that the traumatic situation which Sarah had been subjected to had been the cause of her emotional disturbance. The violence started when she was two years old, and she had been the victim in a 'tug of war' situation between her parents.

Mrs Grant, it seemed, couldn't wait to escape from the home. She remarked:

Being appreciated is nice and I get it at work.

The teacher's perspective

Her teacher, Mrs Jones, saw her as being 'strong-willed and determined'. She realised that Sarah was a very able child but commented that her approach to work could be rather haphazard and inconsistent.

She enjoyed reading and read aloud beautifully with clear expression and intonation. However, she did need to be encouraged to choose appropriate reading material. At one time she was reading adult books brought in from home, the content of which was not considered appropriate for a ten-year-old to read. However, she was persuaded to read other books, notably Jane Austen. She was highly articulate and enjoyed discussion and debate. She had considered views and was able to justify her opinions.

She was a competent mathematician and, if she applied herself, she could be extremely good. Mrs Jones commented:

She has a good problem-solving brain. She has come up with some very interesting ways of solving problems which are different from those of anyone else.

Mrs Jones acknowledged Sarah's relationship problems with peers and adults and doubted whether she was as confident as she appeared:

Sarah worries me because although she comes over as being a flamboyant character, I doubt if she's very sure of herself. She's had such an emotional battering and talks about herself as being calculating and devious. These are strange words for a girl of her age.

Mrs Jones's expectations of Sarah were not high, because her powers of concentration were so poor. Mrs Jones could not see that she would ever apply herself enough to achieve academically. Also she foresaw constant arguments and disputes occurring during Sarah's adult life because of her inability to cooperate with others.

Sarah's story

Sarah reported not liking school because she did not like being shut indoors. She hated rules and was not keen on many subjects at all. However, she did admit to liking maths and problem solving. She felt that the reason she did not excel at English was because her handwriting was not as good as it should be. However, she had lots of ideas for stories and said that she wished she could tape-record them. Drawing was one of her favourite activities both at home and at school. Also she was very fond of history.

She said that she enjoyed reading, usually adventure stories (adult books which tended to be violent), although she did read Jane Austen with a surprising degree of enthusiasm. Sarah said that she was not a popular person and that other people in the class liked getting her into trouble. Sarah's feelings about her relationship with her father were very confused. She rarely saw him, and although she rarely talked about him, she did say that she was sad because he had been posted to Germany and that she would not be able to see him.

The researcher's perspective

Although Sarah was a clever girl, she rarely completed a piece of work. Her powers of concentration were minimal. The trauma which she had experienced had obviously affected her. She seemed unable to form relationships with anyone. When working with a group of other children she was often argumentative. For this reason she was often asked to work alone. Although her teacher did try to befriend and understand her, this had not brought about any lasting change in Sarah.

Perhaps the most striking thing during the interview with Mrs Grant was that she found Sarah extremely difficult to manage. Also what came over very strongly was the mother's depression.

Mrs Grant commented that Sarah didn't like 'fitting in'. Anyone observing her for a morning or so would agree with this statement. Mrs Grant also thought Sarah's self-esteem was high, but it is to be wondered if this was so. It must have been quite obvious to her that other children in the class achieved, while her output of written work was negligible. However, although on the surface she presents a relatively unattractive nature, it is important to note that there had been a lot of discord and trauma in her life.

Mrs Grant described her daughter as being 'materialistic' when she wanted things that other children had as a matter of course. In this she seems to be rather hard on Sarah. It is not unusual for children to want to be on a par with peers in terms of possessions. It was obvious that the family had financial difficulties.

From her own account, Sarah had changed schools on four occasions since starting school. This was not unusual for an army family, but for such a child who had emotional complications to cope with, this could only add to her problems.

Figure 7.2 shows an example of Sarah's written work. It was very difficult to find something she had actually finished and this is a report of a science experiment. Although she did not have a handwriting problem, she did have difficulty with concentration.

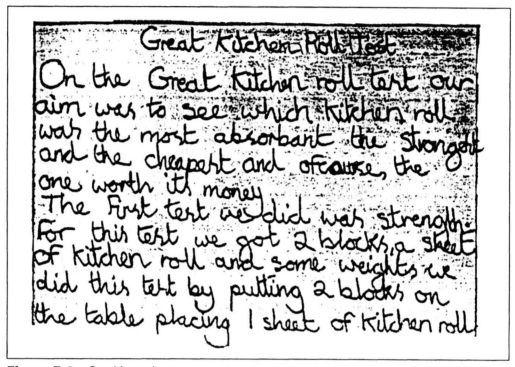

Figure 7.2 Sarah's work

Repertory grids

Sarah's view of Mrs Jones

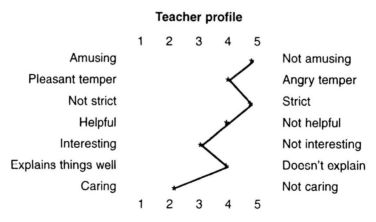

Sarah felt that the following constructs were important for the ideal teacher: he/she should explain things well, be helpful, not strict, amusing, have a pleasant temper, be interesting, be caring. She saw her teacher as being: not amusing, not having a particularly pleasant temper, very strict, not particularly helpful, not explaining things very well, but being reasonably interesting and quite caring.

Mrs Jones's view of Sarah

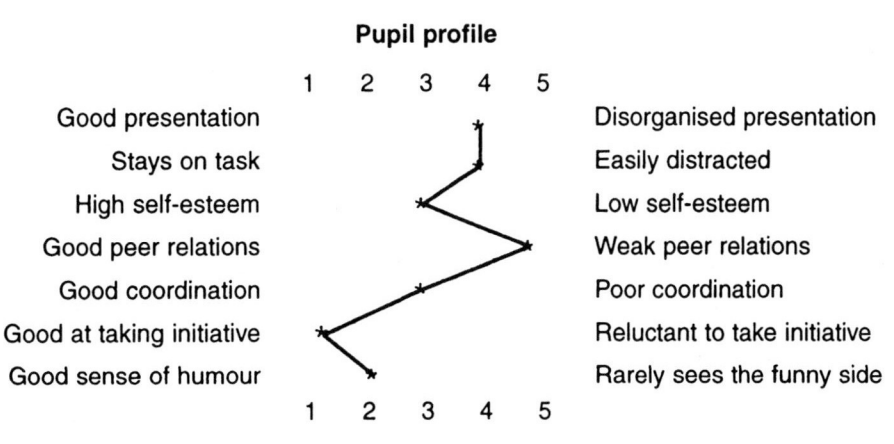

Pupil profile

	1	2	3	4	5	
Good presentation						Disorganised presentation
Stays on task						Easily distracted
High self-esteem						Low self-esteem
Good peer relations						Weak peer relations
Good coordination						Poor coordination
Good at taking initiative						Reluctant to take initiative
Good sense of humour						Rarely sees the funny side

Mrs Jones saw the following constructs as being conducive to achievement: good coordination, good peer relations, the ability to stay on task, good presentation, high self-esteem, the ability to take initiative, having a good sense of humour.

She saw Sarah as having reasonable coordination, weak peer relationships, was easily distracted and had disorganised presentation skills (although her handwriting was not poor). She was seen as having a reasonably high self-esteem and had a good sense of humour. She was also eager to take initiative.

Researcher's comments

Sarah had a low opinion of her teacher, but this was possibly the opinion that she would have of any person who was in authority over her. Her teacher's opinion of Sarah, however, was a little more positive and it was evident from the observation sessions that Mrs Jones did try to help Sarah. Mrs Jones's offers, though, were often rejected.

Alistair

Outline of the child

Alistair was smaller than average, with curly, auburn hair. His father was a sergeant in the army. His mother worked part-time as a special needs assistant in an infant school.

The parents' perspective

Alistair's mother, Mrs Holloway, was interviewed.

Alistair developed at a swift pace during early months. His language development progressed rapidly and he started to read at about three. By the time he started school he was reading fluently. The time and care which had been lavished upon Alistair was explained by his mother:

> Alistair is our second child. Our first died a cot death at two weeks. He was born three years after that, so we've paid an extreme amount of attention to him.

She acknowledged that his main problems were social:

> He can't make friends easily. He tries to take over. If things don't go his way, he gets frustrated.

Perhaps another reason for Alistair not being popular was that he liked to play games which had very involved rules. Mrs Holloway remarked:

> He has lots of theories about how and why games should be played. The other children aren't interested.

She described Alistair as being very inquisitive. He took things apart and rebuilt them and always wanted to know about anyone who came to the house. In addition, he was very articulate and could talk on a variety of subjects. He also had a very mature sense of humour. However, concentration, attention and handwriting were all poor, as his mother commented:

> If an activity includes handwriting, then he'll be distracted within a few minutes.

His self-discipline, according to Mrs Holloway, was not good. He was very reluctant to work unless someone actually stood over him. Also, he did not take criticism well and this usually resulted in a temper tantrum. As far as school was concerned, Alistair apparently liked it:

> Believe it or not, Alistair enjoys coming to school but he doesn't like playtimes because he hasn't bonded with any children.

Mrs Holloway's attitude can be gleaned by what she had to say about Alistair's self-esteem:

> His self-esteem is very poor. He's been knocked down so often, told he's not good, not paying attention, a trouble maker.

From her point of view the school needed to work a lot harder to improve Alistair's social skills and powers of concentration:

> Also he needs to be channelled more into doing the things he's interested in.

As one might expect, Alistair's hobbies were all individual: computers, bird-watching and reading. Mrs Holloway's expectations for Alistair were as follows:

It's got to be his choice. He wants to be a scientist. I would love him to go to a university but I'm not going to push him unless it's what he wants. I'd be content if he just got O levels if he were happy socially.

Neither Mrs Holloway nor her husband went on to higher education straight from school, but Mr Holloway had recently studied for a degree and Mrs Holloway was taking an Access course.

The teacher's perspective

Alistair's teacher, Mrs Dowling, had done as much as she possibly could to integrate him into the class. As she said:

Alistair has potential but it's so sad and frustrating [that he doesn't work]. It must be so for him, he must realise. Other children I've taught who have had high ability, have an insatiable appetite to succeed, are very much on top of things, are organised, can concentrate, can channel that ability. That isn't Alistair. Highly able children can complete, meet deadlines and handle things well. Alistair undoubtedly has that ability but he can't channel it.

Like Alistair's mother, Mrs Dowling thought that Alistair's biggest problems were social. She explained:

The other children don't like him because he's so selfish. He's got a very big ego. He finds sharing very difficult. All children find it difficult but by Year 6 they've developed strategies to control the urge to have everything themselves, they've learnt to share. Alistair hasn't.

When working in a group, he found it difficult to accept other points of view. He wanted to hold all the equipment. If he could not, he became aggressive. When Alistair was unable to have attention, his behaviour deteriorated. Discussion times were very difficult:

He's at his worst when we're all sitting on the carpet talking. Unless he's allowed to be centre stage and to do the talking, he becomes disruptive.

She went on to compare his social behaviour with that of her own six-year-old son and was convinced that their maturity levels were on a par. She felt that he was not disciplined at all at home. In fact she had witnessed a scene whereby Alistair had been lunging at his younger brother with a huge golfing umbrella, in a very dangerous manner. Instead of removing the umbrella and speaking to him severely, his mother said weakly, 'Oh Alistair, put it down'. Of course he continued. In Mrs Dowling's opinion, this was a clear example of a breakdown in discipline.

Alistair had a home/school booklet in which his teacher could report upon his daily behaviour and work. His parents were invited to make their comments. The comments from home about the way he was handled were very negative. In fact the school was criticised so heavily that an interview was arranged between the headteacher, Alistair's teacher and Mrs Holloway. Alistair's parents had always wanted special treatment for him but his teacher thought it was time that he was treated in the same way as other children:

> I think his mother wants to perpetuate too much the 'special case' aspect for Alistair. I would like to push for Alistair to have time to breathe. I think she's hovering over him too much. I think there's a case for normalising him.

Mrs Dowling reported that Alistair was extremely interested in science and would willingly experiment and talk to an adult the whole day, if this were possible. He was highly articulate. However, the moment he was asked to formalise his findings, he lost interest completely. She added:

> Rightly or wrongly we live in a system where at the end of the day, you've got to account for yourself on paper. What a shame that he's got such wonderful ability but no application for written work.

His written work was very messy and his handwriting was described by his teacher as being 'appalling'. He found writing very laborious and wanted action all the time. She felt that one of the reasons that he did not like writing was that he had an obsession with adult attention. If he wrote, he could not talk to an adult. Alistair's attitude towards school, as far as his teacher was concerned, was as follows:

> Strangely enough he's always pleased to see me in the morning. He's cheerful about school. He likes project work and loves doing practical things.

Mrs Dowling thought that Alistair's self-esteem was probably low because his mental energy wasn't being channelled into anything worthwhile.

Alistair's story

Although Alistair was keen to talk about an experiment he'd been doing in the classroom, he was rather reluctant to talk about himself. It was also difficult to involve him in a group discussion. His favourite subjects were maths, science and technology. He said he liked making things and working things out. He 'sort of' liked school but didn't seem as fond of school as his mother or teacher thought. When asked why he became distracted with his work he said:

> Sometimes I tend to chatter to people and this makes me get behind with my work. But it's mainly people chatting to me.

He was asked about friends and he replied sadly:

> I haven't got many. I don't know why.

The researcher's perspective

Alistair's school life had not been easy. He had social difficulties which were not made easier by the constant monitoring of all aspects of school life by his mother. He continually sought adult attention although there was certainly no shortage of that at home. He could also become argumentative and sometimes violent. This had been witnessed during periods of observation.

His mother criticised the school for not trying to improve Alistair's concentration and self-esteem but during observation sessions it became apparent that his teacher had worked hard to improve Alistair's self-esteem and attention span and this had increased to some extent.

Mrs Holloway also said that Alistair should be allowed to follow his own interests. What must be taken into consideration here are the constraints of the National Curriculum which leaves little time for children to follow their own interests. Such interests could however, be built into an enrichment programme.

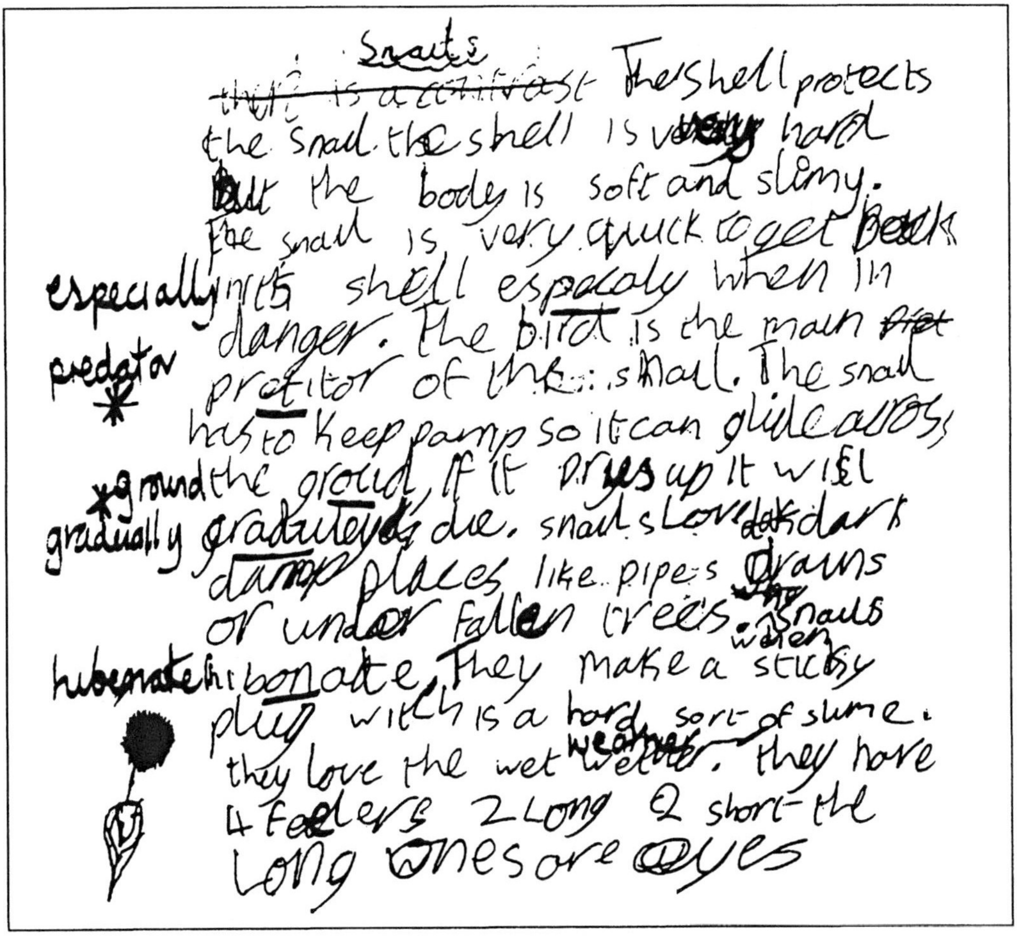

Figure 7.3   Alistair's work

Mrs Holloway was also very critical of the way the school had handled Alistair and had conveyed her feelings to him. This negative attitude had obviously affected him and the way he felt about the school. Possibly there was a link between her criticism of the school and Alistair's inability to conform.

His teacher has said that he was very immature and that his behaviour was at the level of a six-year-old. Naturally other children in the class could not be expected to respond positively to someone whose social development was so different from their own. It is interesting that Alistair put the blame for his distraction on other people.

However, in Alistair's favour, it must be said that he was not receiving any specialist help at the time of the research from any agency outside the school for his 'appalling' handwriting or for his behaviour (help had been available in the past in that he had been referred to an educational psychologist). Having said that though, his teacher and headteacher did give him a lot of time, attention and support.

Figure 7.3 shows an example of Alistair's work, taken from an exercise book, and it is easy to appreciate his problems with handwriting.

Repertory grids

Alistair's view of Mrs Dowling

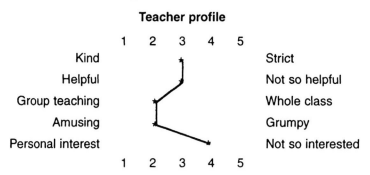

Alistair's choice of constructs showed that he liked a teacher to be amusing, to teach in groups as opposed to the whole class, to be kind, helpful and to take a personal interest in him. He saw Mrs Dowling as not being particularly interested in him although she was reasonably kind, helpful, amusing and taught groups for the majority of the time.

Mrs Dowling's view of Alistair

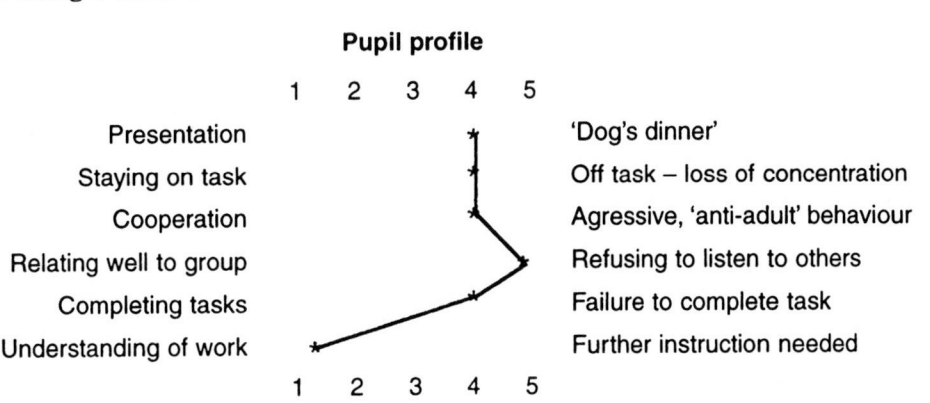

Pupil profile

	1	2	3	4	5	
Presentation				✶		'Dog's dinner'
Staying on task				✶		Off task – loss of concentration
Cooperation				✶		Agressive, 'anti-adult' behaviour
Relating well to group					✶	Refusing to listen to others
Completing tasks				✶		Failure to complete task
Understanding of work	✶					Further instruction needed

Mrs Dowling felt that the following attributes were conducive to achievement: presentation, staying on task, cooperation, relating well to peers in a group situation, completion of work and understanding of work.

On only one of these attributes did Alistair score highly, the understanding of work. His presentation was poor, he found it difficult to stay on task, he was uncooperative and at times exhibited aggressive, anti-adult behaviour, he did not relate well to a group of children and refused to accept the views of others either by dominating or withdrawing. Most of the time he failed to complete items of work.

Researcher's comment

Alistair's assessment of his teacher seems neither wholly positive nor wholly negative, although he definitely felt that she didn't take much of an interest in him. Possibly Alistair saw all adults as trying to exert pressure on him, as his mother did. Mrs Dowling's assessment of Alistair, on the other hand, was poor but he did have a very good understanding of the work she had set. It was noticeable during observation sessions that Mrs Dowling did try to cooperate with Alistair but his immaturity often spoilt this.

A comparison of three under-achieving able children

All these children were under-achieving for different reasons. Fergus's under-achievement can be linked to his poor handwriting and to his need for peer acceptance. He had a supportive home background while Sarah's home life was very different. Her traumatic early years had affected her ability to concentrate and her capacity for forming lasting relationships with others. Alistair had similar social problems which were possibly exacerbated by over-anxious parents. All three under-achievers had difficulties with concentration and had great problems with finishing tasks. Both boys found handwriting laborious and this added to their reluctance to work.

From the five children discussed in Chapters 6 and 7, it can be seen that achievement and under-achievement are the result of a combination of factors and that this combination is rarely the same for each child. The next chapter discusses how the class teacher can get to know such children better and how, in this way, he/she can help them to make the most of themselves despite problems which may not be readily resolved.

Chapter 8

Able Children and the School

General considerations

Research can be informative in many ways but for the classroom teacher it must point to practical approaches to dealing with problems if it is to be of any use. The research reported in the previous chapters has shown that certain motivational forces must be present before a child's potential can be realised. Not only must a child possess ability, but this must be fostered by environmental factors and self-motivation if the child is to succeed. The recommendations presented by Freeman (1979) seem apposite. To reiterate, the child who has the following will be successful:

- parental support which doesn't put too much pressure on the child to achieve;
- freedom from domestic stress;
- the appropriate encouragement and teaching at school;
- no obligation to conform to the average but freedom to develop in his/her own way;
- encouragement to make his/her own decisions and discoveries and respect for his/her abilities.

As can be seen from the above, the part of the parent is of utmost importance.

Parental support

Parents are crucial to the enhancement of ability, as Bloom's research (1985) showed and as supported by the Lee-Corbin study reported earlier. However, care must be taken that enthusiasm for the child to achieve does not put too much pressure on the child as this may result in under-achievement.

Lack of parental support may be the result of a number of circumstances, including marital breakdown or the parent feeling inadequate academically, and thus unable to support the child. The latter might be counteracted by workshops specially designed to help parents to appreciate the problems of an able child, for instance. There could be sections within parent–teacher meetings where parents could be given advice on how to support children who seem to be particularly able. These would be self-selecting and unsupportive parents would not have to be publicly identified. Parental support on behalf of the school could be a positive influence on parent–teacher rapport. As practising teachers we are aware that our jobs can be made easier if we have a good relationship with parents.

Good parent–teacher rapport

A good relationship between parents and teachers is desirable for a child's achievement and every effort should be made to ensure that teachers and parents work together for the good of the child. The teacher, as a professional, can do much to persuade the parents of the value of their support. If parents and teachers are working together for a common goal – the good of the child – then life becomes less difficult for all concerned. It is a sad indictment that so many parents in this study felt 'apologetic' when meeting with teachers. A positive affirmation of the parents' right to be concerned and of the school and parents' joint responsibility would go a long way to ameliorating such a situation.

Teacher support

Support for teachers includes helping them to gain an understanding of the problems faced by the able child. This can only be accomplished with additional teacher education. It is encouraging that so many LEAs are now in the process of publishing or have published guidelines for the education of the able (NAGC, 1995). Freeman (1993) stated that 35 of the 108 authorities in Britain have at least one person responsible for the highly able. This indicated that such support was not widespread, although it is now growing.

Similarly, the 1992 HMI survey had found that only a small core of LEAs had long-established provision for the able. The most effective provision was found in LEAs in which concentrated and well-planned support had been offered by the advisory or inspection service, so it is clear that agencies outside the individual school have a part to play.

During the time in which this research took place, there was so much on the agenda for change for example: changes in the content of the National Curriculum; the introduction of teacher appraisal; the establishment of Local Management of Schools. The result of the latter was that schools had limited resources available for advisory and support services. In fact, the needs of the able were not seen by many as an essential item.

It seems, though, that the education climate for able children is gradually changing. The NACE/DfE project has made great strides in this direction with its regional conferences and 1997 saw the publication of a number of LEA handbooks on guidance for supporting able children, at least a small step in educating the educators.

Although support for able children is essential if they are to fulfil their potential, teachers and parents have to be aware of indicators of under-achievement for it is children who are able but not overtly expressing that ability who are most at risk.

Indicators of under-achievement

An interesting point which many teachers made about achieving children is that they appear eager to please and that they conform. In other words, they fit the teachers' model of what they think an achieving able child should be. Perhaps the child who does not conform to their model is not seen as being able at all. It is all too easy in a busy classroom to prejudge children and to label particular children as average or below.

Early identification of under-achievement is essential if a child's potential is not to be lost. Indicators of under-achievement, noticeable in the child, may be: poor motivation; poor concentration; rarely finishes work set; emotional problems; specific learning difficulties, notably handwriting. The criteria used in the selection of the under-achieving children in the Lee-Corbin study also deserve to be mentioned here. Under-achieving able children often exhibit a vast gap between oral and written work – oral work being superior – but have superior comprehension and retention of concepts, at least when they are interested. Also, they often achieve at or below the average expectation level for their year group. All these factors need to be noted by parents and teachers if children are not to be at risk of under-achievement.

It is worth reiterating Whitmore's (1980) suggestion that under-achieving able children need to enjoy rewarding intellectual stimulation and a sense of 'genuine success' through, for example, debating, scientific experiments and so on, with peers of the same advanced mental age.

There are various ways of overcoming problems which under-achieving and achieving children may encounter and these are considered in the next section.

Strategies for the able

The 1992 HMI survey had also found able children to be unchallenged by work set. In some respects the schools participating in this study were not catering for the needs of the able children. Education programmes had not been drawn up to meet their particular needs, both academic and social, and none of them had been provided with individual programmes. Only one child was visited by a specialist teacher, and that on only three occasions, with no ongoing change in support for the child.

Although the National Curriculum should present a truly differentiated approach, it may still restrict the ablest children because teachers may concentrate on teaching to the prescribed standards of assessment and not beyond them. The National Curriculum is a foundation to which should be added opportunities for extension and enrichment. In this way provision for the able can be specified and developed.

There are certain curriculum strategies that are appropriate in the education of able children: differentiation, enrichment/extension and acceleration. These were discussed in Chapter 3 but we mention them again here to add emphasis.

1. *Differentiation* is essential for all children in a class of mixed ability. It is worth pointing out that an able child is just as entitled to time with the teacher as any other child. It is the nature of the tasks for able children that should differentiate them from those set for other children in the class, in that they should display greater complexity and depth. They should also encourage the use of higher order thinking skills. Teachers may find a recently published book, Quinn's *Critical Thinking in Young Minds* of use in this respect (Quinn, 1997). It gives practical suggestions on how to develop critical thinking in small group situations.

2. *Enrichment/extension* is another curriculum strategy which is desirable for all children. Able children, though, need the opportunity to become intellectually involved in solving problems so they might add depth and breadth to their knowledge and skills. Enrichment opportunities should be carefully planned and fully integrated into the curriculum, rather than 'bolted on' to keep the child occupied.

   Although the National Curriculum places time constraints on the school timetable and may prevent a child's personal interests being followed through in school time, this strategy has been successfully used in America by such people as Renzulli (1996) and Whitmore (1980). It has been particularly successful in helping to reverse under-achievement and increasing self-esteem. When mentoring is required in this context parents may be particularly useful if they have skills and interests which coincide with those of the child and if they are willing to devote time and energy in developing the child's knowledge and expertise. This would have the additional benefit of increasing school/parent collaboration in helping the child to develop his/her full potential.

3. *Acceleration*, by giving a child the opportunity to learn with older children, may be appropriate for some children and can be successful. A recent British study (Hymer and Harbron, 1998) found that early transfer to secondary school was beneficial for some children, especially those from small rural primary schools. However, it is not suitable for all children and the authors caution parents and teachers to familiarise themselves with the broad span of issues surrounding the area of early transfer. The child has to be mature emotionally as well as intellectually if it is to be effective.

Another option is accelerating the child for individual subjects, for example a Year 4 child who is particularly good at maths may be able to join a Year 6 class for that subject. All these strategies should be available for children and teachers, to be utilised when appropriate, although it is realised that there are implications for the structuring and coordination of the whole school curriculum. There are also issues related to the singling out of such children which may in itself cause problems about which parents and teachers need to be sensitive.

A theme which recurs throughout the literature and is supported by the research of Lee-Corbin is the need to nurture ability. If able children were identified at an early stage, then those who needed it could be given additional assistance to overcome difficulties and fewer would under-achieve. It is in an enriched environment, where enrichment is appropriate to the needs of each child, and which fosters the development of motivation, that children will blossom.

However, children are not always what they seem. It became apparent during the research that there were always reasons underlying particular behaviour and that it is incumbent on a teacher to know his/her pupils well if they are to understand these reasons. This was also emphasised by the children who took part in the study. They wanted their teachers to take a personal interest in them. What appears on the surface is not to be taken at face value: for example an achieving child is not always the happy, fulfilled person he/she may seem. Some children may need help in socialising because they are seen as or consider themselves to be 'different'. Other children go to great lengths to hide their ability in order to gain peer acceptance. Such children will be helped if the ethos of the school emphasises that it is 'OK to be bright', while parents too might be encouraged by such an approach.

In addition, the child who displays talent verbally but is not motivated to put pen to paper is not necessarily lazy; there may be other factors involved. A teacher must become alert to certain indicators of under-achievement.

There is no doubt that under-achieving children are difficult to identify. A teacher has to be very sensitive to the way children handle language, assimilate new ideas and concepts and of their approach to problem solving. If a child displays talent in just one aspect but is not an achiever, then he/she is worthy of further investigation. Their abilities in some respects may be masking a specific learning difficulty with the result that they perform at the level of an average child so eluding special attention.

Standardised tests can help to identify such children, especially those who hide their ability deliberately for peer group acceptance. However, tests do have their limitations, for instance some can be culturally biased, and must therefore be chosen carefully. Further, a test is one measurement taken at one particular time; it is a snapshot and we are all aware that sometimes these do not show us at our best. Observation which takes place over time can be more informative and accurate so a combination of both methods would be the better option.

The study has displayed to us that not all children are treated equally with regard to school resources. A school should in theory and in principle cater fairly for the educational needs of all its pupils. The argument that able children will survive unaided because of their ability is flawed as has been observed by a number of researchers (Freeman, 1979; Eyre and Fuller, 1993; George, 1995; Lee-Corbin, 1996) They need education which includes a high level of challenge if they are not to 'give up' in one way or another. Without recognition of their ability and a programme which is designed particularly to meet their needs, not only will they not reach their potential, but they may accumulate other difficulties for themselves and others. For instance a child subjected to inappropriate education may become disaffected; this in turn may link with relationship problems or stimulate difficult behaviour in the classroom or at home.

The research diary compiled during Lee-Corbin's study concludes with the following:

In my practice as a teacher, there are a number of personal changes I would like to make.

1. To attempt to support and guide parents to the best of my ability in the following ways:

   a) To establish a closer rapport with parents, giving advice on how parents can support children educationally. Some parents may need counselling so that their aspirations for their children are set at a higher level.

   b) To make parents aware of certain associations such as the National Association for Gifted Children (NAGC) which support and guide parents. At venues throughout the country, a series of activities are arranged, including talks for parents and whole day educational sessions for children on a variety of subjects. Schools could help to make these facilities more widely known to parents.

2. To provide support and guidance for teachers within the area in which I work:

   a) Teachers' awareness needs to be raised about the specific aspects of teaching able children, about their potential problems and about how to identify such children. This includes not only recognising in children factors associated with under-achievement, but also fostering an alertness to those children who hide their ability to gain peer acceptance.

   b) To bring about a review of policies in schools in which I am associated to allow for the implementation of curriculum strategies such as individual differentiation, enrichment and acceleration.

Not every teacher needs to engage in personal research to learn about these things as most of the above could be accomplished through in-service courses. Recently the National Association for Able Children in Education (NACE), centrally funded, organised a series of in-service courses which were available nation-wide. A number of booklets connected with this project, which give advice to teachers on aspects of teaching concerning the able, are in the process of publication. Another organisation offering such courses is the Brunel Able Children's Education Centre, launched in November 1995 and situated at Brunel University, Twickenham Campus.

There is a need for more specifically trained teachers to support colleagues in the education of able children. It is only when the needs of the able child receive greater public acclaim that this will become possible, because priorities have to be made in restricted budgets. Many of the recommendations in the foregoing do require added expenditure, which could well be considered investment for the future, but the research study did find examples of less financially demanding practices which could be emulated more widely to good effect. These are discussed in the notes below.

Observational notes

During the course of the research a number of excellent teachers were observed and examples are included here of such good practice. Some of these examples may seem obvious and part and parcel of everyday classroom life. This may be so for most children but the able child is sometimes neglected in these respects, at time being deliberately not noticed or praised. This may be for egalitarian reasons and for fear that any attention given to an able child may smack of elitism. Examples of strategies not found to be conducive to achievement in able children are to be found in Appendix B.

Taking a personal interest in individual children

Teacher praising the child for the effort being put into the work

Example 1: One teacher praised Cary for the quality of her English work saying her choice of vocabulary was very colourful which made her work enjoyable to read.

Example 2: Gary was praised for the accuracy of his mathematics assignment and the presentation, even though this was not unusual for him.

Example 3: Richard was praised for the unusual ideas that he had had for solving a problem, and this was discussed with the rest of the class.

Teacher allowing time for child to present his/her work to the class

Example 1: Orlando had written a story which had been made into a book and he read this to the class. This was an amusing story which was extremely well presented and illustrated. His teacher was obviously very pleased.

Example 2: Zara had written a cautionary tale, one about being tempted to take something not belonging to her. This she read to the class, to everyone's enjoyment.

Example 3: As part of the topic on St Lucia, the children had to keep a diary. In this they had to recount their feelings as particular events occurred, including shipwreck. Bryony's account was well written and it had entailed a great deal of thought and imagination. This was read to the class.

Teacher taking time to laugh and joke with the child

Example 1: One teacher arranged a weekly joke telling session at the beginning of the story period, the last session of the day. This lasted for approximately five minutes and was very popular with all the children.

Example 2: In one observation session the teacher became aware that a group of children were giggling. The children were busy writing up and illustrating topic work. One child had attempted to draw a horse and this had convulsed the whole table into helpless laughter – including the artist. Although the teacher wished to stop the giggling, she could not resist joining in, which built on her rapport with the children. One able child in the group seemed to appreciate particularly this sense of camaraderie.

Teacher taking time to talk over difficulties

Example 1: The class was studying plant life and were asked to take quadrats onto the school field. By placing them onto the field, they would be able to count the different numbers of plants within that particular area. Ralph seemed to have difficulties and his teacher devoted a considerable amount of time helping him and talking about the plants in the area of the field he had chosen. He appreciated this special attention, perhaps especially as he rarely needed it.

Example 2: The class was studying geometry and had just started to use protractors. Initially Eleanor had difficulty manipulating the protractor but with help and time taken by the teacher to talk over difficulties, these were dispelled.

Example 3: As a problem-solving exercise, a group of able children were trying to decide where they should set up their camp on a desert island. They had to look at the terrain of the island and the dangers, i.e. wild beasts, availability of drinking water and so on. The ideas which the children thought up were varied but lacking in logical organisation. The teacher took the time to help them sort out their thoughts and then they were better able to find a solution to their problem.

Giving the children time to express their views

Example 1: Before writing a book review on a book which had been read to the class (*Hydra* by Robert Swindells), the children were asked to discuss the book, i.e. what they liked or disliked about it, the characters, the plot and so on. This formed a general class discussion in which each child was listened to with respect.

Example 2: The children had been studying the Tudors and they were planning to dramatise the story of Henry and his wives. The children were asked to discuss in groups how they were to do this and what were the most important parts to be included in a limited amount of time. After ten minutes they were asked to gather together to pool their ideas. Each group was allowed to present their opinions in a supportive atmosphere.

Example 3: Classroom rules in one school were determined by teachers and children working together. During class discussion, the children were asked to present their opinions on what the classroom rules should be and why. In this way it was thought that they were more likely to be kept. Everyone's opinion was given consideration and it was clear that each child felt that his/her ideas were valued.

Planning lessons to cater for the needs of able children

Well-planned lessons with instructions to the children clearly conveyed

Example 1: One lesson was based on Kit Wright's poem *The Magic Box*. Each child had a copy of the poem and the meaning was discussed. Each child had to produce a similar poem using their own thoughts about what should be kept in this box and lastly they had to describe the box. These instructions were clear and explicit and produced good results from all the children who seemed to work to the best of their ability.

Example 2: One mathematics lesson involved the children constructing 3-D mathematical shapes. The children had to construct a net and from this had to cut out and then glue their shape. The step-by-step instructions were conveyed to the children in a precise and unambiguous manner. The able children were encouraged to go on to make shapes which were more complicated once they had finished making a simple shape.

Example 3: A group of children were conducting an experiment on friction. They were provided with a number of different materials and had to determine the force, using a spring balance, which had to be exerted to pull a toy truck plus weight on different surfaces over a given distance. The children coped well with this and were able to draw conclusions from their individual experiments, no matter what challenging surfaces were introduced by the able children.

Allowing children to work with others of similar ability to enable them to exchange ideas and to be mutually supportive

Example 1: Children were allowed to collaborate with another child to write and illustrate a book which became part of the school library. These books were written for a younger audience, i.e. for Years 3 and 4, and were very successful, which gave scope for the able children to use their imaginations.

Example 2: In order to help the children to think through the concept of bullying, they were put into small groups and presented with various situations which were to be discussed. Later they had to talk through what they felt about these situations with the whole class. One group decided to act out their situation. There were certainly differences between the groups in terms of quality of output but the able children appeared to gain from being grouped together because they were able to 'bounce' ideas off each other.

Example 3: Two children were allowed to work together on a particularly complex mathematics problem concerning the best way to stock a supermarket. The discussion which arose from this was lively and it was evident that it had helped to create a number of ideas which they tried out in order to find the solution.

The above examples will have struck a familiar chord with the majority of teachers and they are provided as illustrations or to stimulate ideas for specific classroom work. However, there is one item which is essential for a school if the aim is to make better provision for able children, and that is a policy. Eyre (1997) has reported on this area in detail and therefore it will only be covered here briefly. The following is based in part on her excellent book *Able Children in Ordinary Schools*.

A policy for the more able

Within each school such a policy should be seen as a working document, subject to change and review, while it needs to be coordinated by an enthusiast. It should also be borne in mind that a policy will only be accepted if all the staff agree with what has been decided and are prepared to make changes. It is important that the focus is not only academic ability and how it must be fostered. Other talents also need consideration, for instance art, music, drama and sport need to be taken into account.

In writing a policy for the able child the following aspects need to be considered.

1. General rationale

• Why such a policy is needed.
• Where it links into general school aims and philosophy.

2. Aims

What the school aims to provide for able pupils, e.g.:
• entitlement to appropriate education;
• work at higher cognitive levels;
• opportunities to develop specific skills or talents;
• a concern for the whole child – social and intellectual.

3. Definitions

How ability might be defined was discussed in Chapter 1 but the view that is generally accepted is that ability is multi-dimensional (Gardner, 1983).

4. General overall approach

For example, in-class provision, setting, withdrawal and how this is to be accomplished.

5. Identification and monitoring schemes

Identification

This should be based on teacher assessment and judgement including analysis of information from any other schools which the child has attended and consultations with the child, parents and colleagues.

Although each school will want to develop its own, the criteria used for the current research is presented here as an example.

The achievers exhibited all or most of the following traits:
- in general classwork, the child achieves at a level well above the average expectation level for that year group;
- generally work is complete and well done;
- he/she has superior comprehension and retention of concepts;
- he/she is articulate and this command of English is shown in written work.

The under-achievers exhibited all or most of the following traits:
- in general classwork, the child achieves at or below the average expectation level for that year group;
- he/she frequently hands in work that is incomplete or poorly done;
- he/she has superior comprehension and retention of concepts when interested;
- he/she exhibits a vast gap between oral and written work.

Monitoring

How is progress to be monitored?

Some schools prefer to use individual needs profiles. These should:
- list individual needs;
- be available for planning work;
- be readily accessible for those concerned.

6. Organisational responses

- Acceleration – skipping a year, setting, acceleration for particular subjects.
- Withdrawal across year groups.
- Provision for exceptional pupils, e.g. mentoring.

7. In-class approach

- Enrichment/extension – planning: the relevance of material to the whole class needs to be considered as does the most significant needs of the able child so that, relevant activities can be devised and set realistic goals set.

Openings for extension and open-ended work might include:
- working with others of like ability;
- differentiation;
- challenge within subject areas.

8. Out-of-class activities

- Enrichment days. These usually include a visit to a place of interest or a day spent engaging in activities which are outside classroom based experience and which add to particular fields of study.
- A variety of school clubs. Consider whether it is worthwhile sharing expertise in one school with those in a cluster group.
- The same applies to musical and sporting opportunities within your school.

9. Personal and social education

The children discussed in Chapters 6 and 7 emphasise how important this is. The child's overall development has to be considered, not just an exceptional skill or talent which they possess. Children may need help in evaluating their self-esteem, developing moral values and learning how to relate to others. They may also need guidance in organising themselves. Peer group relationships have to be monitored with care, as the children are often vulnerable when adults are no longer around. Early identification and intervention at the beginning of a child's schooling can encourage cooperative rather than competitive behaviour between children.

10. Responsibility for monitoring and coordinating progress

For example, a named coordinator or class teacher. If a named person is personally responsible for coordinating able child provision within a school, this ensures that the needs of the able are consistently part of the school's agenda. Whenever subject areas are discussed, the coordinator raises the implications for the most able in that subject. That person is also able to review the progress of identified pupils with individual staff and to keep staff informed of current thinking.

11. Process for review and development

- How often is this policy and its effectiveness to be reviewed?
- Is it to be reviewed by the staff as a whole or by a staff working party?

- Responsibilities: e.g. class teachers to be responsible for maintaining the documentation of pupils' progress; able needs coordinator to check a sample of pupil records to ensure that records are being kept.

12. Use of outside agencies for training provision

For example, LEA courses.

Using the results of the research reported in earlier chapters as a springboard, this chapter has provided a range of examples for individual teachers and whole schools to draw on for ensuring better provision for able children. These are intended to act as stimuli for new ideas or to be adapted to suit individual contexts and needs rather than to be used as templates for action. The importance of tailoring action to each special case is further emphasised in the next chapter, which looks more closely at classroom life and how a teacher can get to know just how a child ticks.

Chapter 9

Exploring the Classroom Situation

At the beginning of this book we alluded to the philosophy which underpinned the research described in subsequent chapters (Lee-Corbin, 1996). This included a concern to represent adequately the complexity of the lived situation for the participants, including the teachers, the parents and the children themselves. Thus a naturalist, holist approach was chosen to do justice to the multitude of perspectives present. Further, this allowed us, and then readers, to recognise that part of the complexity of the situation lies in the dynamic interaction of these perspectives. Understandings and misunderstandings of each others' views, intentions and actions form the basis for both action and achievement.

This chapter explores this aspect further, firstly by explaining some of the ways in which individual's understandings can be illuminated in research using personal construct theory approaches. Next some examples of these understandings and how they contribute to interpersonal interactions are discussed. Finally, some suggestions are provided so that readers, particularly teachers, can make use of the techniques to get to know children better and so be in a better position to help them achieve their latent potential.

Recognising and exploring other worlds

There is no need to study an academic treatise to get a feel for the main tenets of the theory supporting personal construct approaches. A thought experiment will suffice to give the flavour of its main propositions.

> *Imagine standing on a hilltop looking out over the countryside. Further, imagine that you are a farmer contemplating your land. What catches your attention? What is important for you in what you see? How do you interpret some of the specific things you see?*
>
> *Now, blink hard and look at the scene again, but this time as an artist planning a picture. Ask yourself those same questions again.*
>
> *And for good measure, blink hard once again and examine the landscape from the point of view of a property developer, again thinking through the questions.*

When we and others tried this we found the 'farmer' in us focusing on such things as the kinds of crops that were growing or the animals that were feeding off the land. We thought about the fertility and drainage of the soil and how we might improve it. We wondered if it was time to plant or harvest.

The 'artist', on the other hand, concentrated on appreciating light and shade, colour and texture, wondering how to capture form and structure, intensity and subtlety.

Our 'property developer' had different interests and concerns. The accessibility of the land, how it could be subdivided into plots or reshaped to make room for more units predominated these thoughts.

So what do these mental exercises tell us? First we can recognise readily that different roles, motives and experience, among other things, lead us to deem some things more important than others even though the object of our attention remains the same. Indeed, some things may be ignored or not noticed at all, depending on where we are 'coming from'. Other things will be interpreted differently. Friable soil may be the farmer's joy and the property developer's problem. The action that such interpretations lead us to is, of course, equally diverse. We may seem to inhabit the same world, but each of us construes it differently.

We may take as an example two of the children we met in Chapters 6 and 7, Harriet and Fergus. Both are able children with supportive family backgrounds who are members of the same school class, yet it is clear from their stories that they view their intellectual ability differently. As a consequence, how they interact with others in the classroom and how they demonstrate that ability indicates that, for all intents and purposes, they inhabit different worlds. We might wonder how that has come to be.

Personal construct theory, through the seminal work of George Kelly (1955), provides us with some possible explanations. He suggested that people form hypotheses about the world from their experience and use these to predict future experiences. As they progress through their lives these hypotheses are continually being put to the test and sometimes they are revised if they are frequently proved wrong or inadequate. To take a simple example to start with, if children in their early years in the home environment are frequently praised for exploring and finding answers, something which they find rewarding anyway, they build a set of hypotheses, or *constructs*, about the world that encourages them to continue with such behaviour. This will be especially so if other family members behave in the same way towards the world with success. The children continue to construe themselves as explorers and answer seekers and behave accordingly when they go to school. There they will meet a range of different reactions or challenges to their approaches to the world, from their teachers and their peers. What happens next becomes more complicated. Their constructs about exploring and answer seeking are embedded in a whole array or framework of other constructs about the world (their *construct system* in Kelly's theory). Some of these constructs are more important or central to their being than others (*core constructs*) so they will be less ready to change these than they will other constructs which are more peripheral, more open to challenge and amendment. They may find the natural world fascinating, collecting and prodding insects to see what they will do. When a particular prod results in a sting, some parts of that natural world may be reviewed as less fascinating, more to be avoided.

Individuals have many diverse experiences in their lives and so have different opportunities to test their hypotheses or constructs. Thus they have a range of different constructs, and hence construct systems, while each construct may respond differently to challenge. Just as our farmer/artist/property developer have different experiences of the land in question and various priorities in mind when they view it, so the children have different priorities about their abilities and how they are best put into action. They will stick with some constructs through thick and thin, only put some into action in certain circumstances and change others to meet the challenges.

Our thought experiment also demonstrates other aspects of our construing. One is that individuals sometimes view things in similar ways, based on some common experience. If we have, for instance, some experience of art, even it is not a priority in our lives, we may view the land in similar ways to the artist. The theory calls using similar constructs in a similar way *commonality*. Even though we may not be able to reproduce the scene as the artist does, we may still appreciate its aesthetics in a similar way. Further, although we may not hold the same constructs as the property developer, we might, drawing on our experiences of living in a community, house hunting, needing access to schools and so on, be able to see the world 'through' the constructs of the property developer. The theory calls this process *sociality*. This process of sociality is helped if the property developer can explain clearly to us some of the constructs that are important to him/her. The farmer, too, might be able to see the sense that the property developer or artist makes of the scene, but he/she may not agree with them, or want to put them into any form of action, because the land has different significance for him/her. Constructs related to the land for this person may be imbued with a stronger emotional component, perhaps drawn from years of family commitment to the land.

An old idiom is that beauty is in the eye of the beholder. All our land viewers may construe the scene as beautiful but they may not mean the same thing by it. Therein lies the difficulty of trying to share our constructs through the clumsy medium of language. Personal construct theory, as it has been developed, provides some tools to help us with this (Dalton and Dunnett, 1992).

First, it is suggested that since constructs are related to each other within the construct system we might understand one construct better if we know which other constructs are closely linked to it. For the farmer, beauty and fertility might be closely linked, for instance. Second, constructs are considered to be dimensions along which we rate things, be they objects, people or events. They help us to discriminate between things – some things being more beautiful than others. We can identify things which are similarly beautiful and things which contrast with them that are less so. We can understand other people's constructs better if we encourage them to articulate their description of 'less so'. For the farmer, the contrast description to 'beautiful' may be 'rugged' while for the artist it might be 'bland'. Indeed, for the artist, 'rugged' things might also be beautiful things! The theory provides us with tools to explore further these bipolar dimensions and the links they have with each other. We used some of these in the research described earlier in the book. One such method was the repertory grid, a particularly structured approach useful for research, but there are other less formal ways that teachers and parents could use to get to know their children better, to learn to see the world through their constructs. We will return to these methods in the third part of this chapter but first let us look at how the principles of the theory can be seen in action in the world of the able child.

Living in alternative worlds

As adults we are used to playing many roles, adjusting our behaviour to fit circumstances and recognising that people who interact with us in particular roles see us slightly differently than those who 'know' us in other contexts. When we think about it we see this as 'common sense'. Such common sense is explained in the theory discussed in the previous section by the process of our bringing different constructs to bear with varying priority in different situations, based on our anticipation of those situations learned from experience. Yet, we are frequently surprised when others misconstrue our intent, when two people who we think know us well have different expectations of us or when we find ourselves behaving in some circumstances against the principles we hold by in others. Teachers might contemplate their own examples, but, speaking as psychologists as well as teachers, we can feel uncomfortable in social situations when people expect us to be 'analysing' them all the time. We wonder why our colleagues see us as organised while our partners chide us for disorder. At one and the same time we can readily understand the 'strange' behaviour of our friends' teenage children while despairing of the antics of our own.

Using such experience as an analogy and supporting it with personal construct theory, we can begin to see more clearly some possible reasons why children behave differently at home than they do at school, why some conform to the context and others refuse to, why the teachers' and parents' view of the child may differ and why all these different world views sometimes come in to conflict.

To illustrate this further by drawing on some of the results of our research, we will return to our example of able children entering the world of school. They may find their anticipation confirmed that their questioning of things will be well received, at least by their teachers. One of our teacher respondents recognised that, although such children are sometimes seen as difficult, the professional response should be more constructive:

> [They should have] a teacher who recognises that creative people aren't nuisances. He/she has to create lots of situations and opportunities for the child to think laterally.

Another teacher appreciated that an adequate response to the child incorporated an acknowledgement of the child's developing self as well as the provision of formal learning opportunities:

> A teacher has to be aware of other possibilities within the subject to broaden their [the children's] scope. For success a teacher must also bolster their self-esteem.

Guiding expectations as well as understanding their different approaches to school work was something that another teacher felt was important:

> [The teacher] has to have the ability to motivate them in different ways, to have an understanding of their talents and abilities. Work has to be at the right level and challenging enough for them to do well. Able children know when they're not being challenged enough. You have to let them know what you expect.

Figure 9.1 combines the ideas of all the teachers on our study about what the characteristics were of the ideal teacher of able children.

It is clear from those characteristics that the teacher needs to know and understand each child well if he/she is to set appropriate parameters, motivate and be a source of inspiration to each child. One child might respond to boundaries by pushing against them while another might hide behind them; one child might be inspired by a perfect example while another might find it too high a goal to strive for in an already difficult life.

This demonstrates that the interaction between able children and their teachers is a fundamental issue and we must not forget that the children bring their constructs to the interaction too.

As we saw in Chapter 1, there was some commonality in the expectations that able children had of 'good' teachers. Most appreciated them being amusing but a large majority wanted very much that they were 'interested in me' and showed 'understanding'. We have seen in earlier chapters too that Harriet and Fergus responded to a common school environment and the same teacher in different ways. We could speculate on the individual interactions between the teacher and each of these children, and, indeed, see from the data some of the consequences. However, children do not come into contact with their teachers in isolation. The school is a complex society; other children are engaged in the interactions too.

Both Fergus and Harriet have experienced some of their constructs being supported and others challenged by interactions with their peers. Fergus, at the time of the research, chose to moderate his questioning behaviour to conform to the norm of behaviour as he saw it reflected by his peers. On the other hand, Harriet continued to demand answers and to challenge ideas even though it made her unpopular. She chose to protect her constructs by withdrawing into her books and writing, although it pained her to have few friends. We will explore in the final part of this chapter some ways that teachers might deal with similar situations once they have developed a clearer recognition and understanding of them.

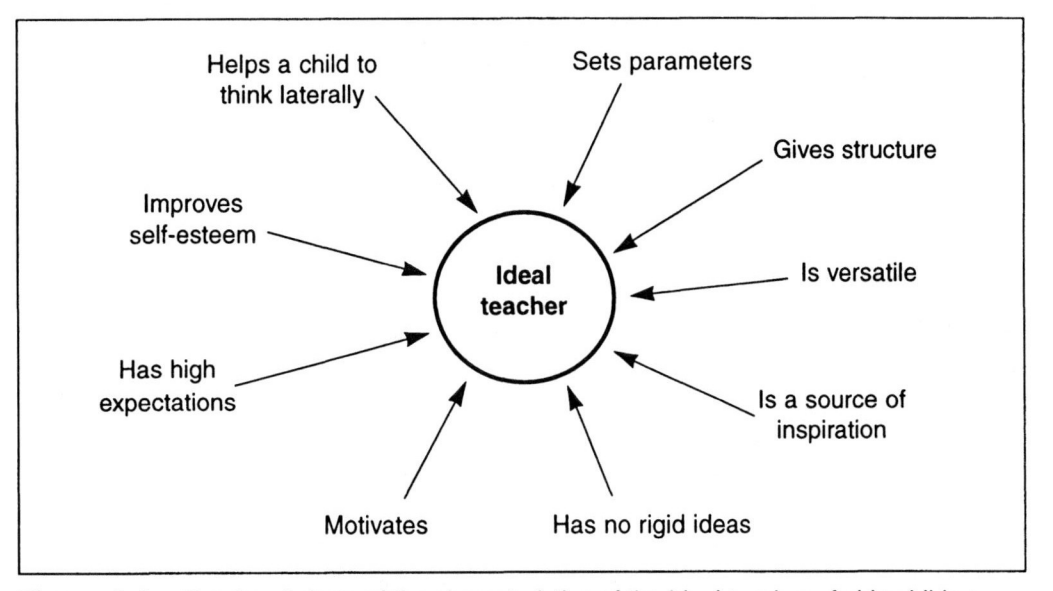

Figure 9.1   Teachers' views of the characteristics of the ideal teacher of able children

Entering the world of able children

In Chapters 6 and 7 we explained how we had explored a particular aspect of each teacher's and each child's world by asking them to consider a sample of representatives of that aspect. How teachers construed able children was explored by their consideration of particular able children while the views of 'good' teachers were elicited by children focusing on teachers they had had experience of. Using a structured repertory grid format, each person construed others as *elements* in the grid by taking three examples and considering how two were similar and different from the third. In this way the two descriptors which describe the dimension of comparison, or *construct*, were brought out, for example good at taking the initiative >>>> reluctant to take the initiative (teacher's construct about children) or strict >>>> not strict (child's construct about teachers).

From our analysis of the grids, looking for groups of matching elements (construed in similar ways) and matching constructs (individuals being rated similarly), we were able to begin to draw up pictures of each person's construct system. For instance, one teacher expects that children who take the initiative will also have high self-esteem. A child has found that strict teachers are neither amusing nor interested in him. We might want to challenge some of those constructs, to help children with low self-esteem take some initiative and to help children see that strictness may not preclude a teacher taking an interest in children, but first we need to know that these views of the world exist.

At this point we will turn to less formal methods for exploring constructs with the children in our care, though we would encourage teachers to spend some time to explore their own constructs about children, able children who do and do not achieve in particular. They may, in this way, clarify their ideas by articulating them but also discover that some hypotheses, which they use to guide their actions, could bear some testing too. It might, for example, be that the class 'show off', rather than being ignored, might be better given more attention in the form of provision of more challenging work in an area which interests him/her.

The simplest and least time-consuming way of finding some clues about how children view their worlds is to become especially alert to how they describe it in their talk and writing. To use some rather simple examples, we might have become acclimatised to the cry 'but its boring', but we could develop a greater understanding of the child's meaning for 'boring' by noticing the other dimensions of activities that are described that way. Are they more frequently things to do with solitary working or working with other children, to do with refining old skills or developing new ones? We might then watch out for the descriptions of things that are not considered boring, perhaps being described as 'needing imagination' or 'can see the point of' (giving a different interpretation of the same word 'boring', you might agree!). Not only will this help us understand the child's meaning but it will provide us with clues about how to interact with him/her better, permutating appropriately for each child, from the example, solitary and group work, creative activities and explanations about how the activity might come in useful.

If we have a little more time with a particular child, the cry 'its boring' could be responded to by questions such as 'what else is boring?' (now that might surprise them!), 'tell me something that isn't boring', 'what is it about that that makes it different to the boring things?' These seem to be easier questions to help a person explore their own ideas than more obvious ones like 'why is it boring?' ('it just is!'), because the comparison or contrast helps bring out the salient aspects.

Both of these approaches involve active listening, paying attention to both what is said and what is not said, especially if we have expectations about what should be said. They also involve suspending for a little while our own understandings of the world and the meanings that we attribute to words. We recognise that in the busy, and sometimes noisy, world of the classroom, this is not easy since we inhabit a similar world of work ourselves. We have, however, found some surprising things when we have made the time to do so.

Other techniques which can be incorporated into class activities or given to children who have completed class work early include using narrative or drawings.

The former has the advantage of allowing the teacher to explore the child's world in their own time, outside the pressure in the busy classroom, while the latter is particularly suitable for young children or those who have difficulty with writing.

For a narrative exploration children can be set the task of describing their ideal and 'nightmare' lessons or school, or perhaps asked to write about one occasion when they enjoyed something enormously and another when they have been miserable. The task should be defined by what aspect of the child's world concerns or interests the teacher most and is only limited by the teacher's imagination. It is important to remember to include the contrast notion in the activity whether it be in the form of a story or a picture.

For the latter, the task of drawing a picture of a time 'when I was bored' and one 'when I wasn't' could be set, or 'a situation I like to be in and one I would avoid being in' perhaps for older children. Of course, all may very likely not be revealed in the picture itself, but much may come from asking the child 'what's going on here?' By encouraging children to talk about their pictures and the story they represent we are often granted insights into parts of their worlds that they would find difficult to put into words otherwise.

For very young children, or those of us whose views of our own drawing or writing skills constrain us, objects can also be stimulants to sharing construing. The child might be asked to gather together some toys, some that are favourite and others they are not so keen on. These then form the focus for exploring what is good about the favourites compared with the rejects, what can be done with the former and not the latter, which is best and why.

We have tried to keep our suggestions here relatively simple so that they might be more easily incorporated into the practical world of the classroom. However, we must at this point introduce two caveats. The first is to warn readers, tongue in cheek, that once they are alert to constructs they will begin to see them everywhere, and their own will begin to pop up unsolicited. While explaining about using toys the writer of the chapter began a train of thought about explaining in writing compared with giving an explanation in a workshop. She had some preference for the latter because, for example, she could provide different forms of explanation when people look puzzled or introduce some humour when they seem tired. On the other hand, drafting and redrafting a chapter, though tedious, has other advantages – but we won't go into that lest we reveal too many personal constructs and have to do something about them!

This leads to the second and more serious caveat. Revealing one's own constructs or gaining insights into those of others is only a first step. Information on which to base decisions and action is provided but the decision and action still has to be made. Where a problem exists, for instance a child who appears to be under-achieving, more information about how they view learning and their school world may be useful and illuminating but it is not the solution in itself, only a guide to action.

Once we have that information, or some of it, though, we can made more informed decisions about what action to take, perhaps selecting the most appropriate ones from those found in the literature, as described in Chapter 2. To provide one example here, a teacher may discover that a child, considered to be able but not as yet achieving his/her potential, has concerns about 'never being as good as the high flyers' in the class, can cope too easily with some activities which are 'boring' but struggles with others which 'make me feel so stupid', but frequently plays down any special ability to fit in with the norm of the rest of the class. This teacher might consider Whitmore's (1980) recommendations to be useful here. We have expanded on these from the results of our own research and experience and the suggestions include grouping under-achievers together for their work so that they might:

1. decrease self-degrading comparisons with high achievers;
2. develop acceptance of self through acceptance of others with similar problems;
3. enjoy rewarding intellectual stimulation;
4. enjoy a sense of 'genuine success' through working with peers of the same advanced mental age.

Teachers might also:

5. allow frequent opportunities for them to enter into discussion/debate with other children on given topics when, for example, a lack of expertise in writing would not matter;
6. provide plenty of scope for problem-solving activities (again although this may call for the minimum of writing skills, in a group activity one person could act as scribe);
7. use methods which are flexible and open-ended so that children are encouraged to use their creativity, can work at their own pace and achieve different but relevant goals;
8. introduce the children to higher order thinking skills as discussed in Chapter 8 (Quinn, 1997);
9. use mentors, if possible, to help the children with their particular interests (parents who are willing to give a little time are often helpful for this);
10. celebrate the children's successes;
11. most important of all, value their opinions and ideas.

Summary

Let us review here what we have learnt from personal construct theory that might be of use to teachers coping with able children in their classrooms.

As individuals, teachers or children, we all approach situations with our constructs at the ready. These are anticipations which combine cognitive and emotional aspects with a readiness to act in a particular way which we deem appropriate given our prior experiences of similar situations. These constructs are important because they have allowed us to survive so far. Some of them, though, may be less useful than others for they prevent us seeing that the situation is subtly different from what we expect. Others might be downright disadvantaging because they bring prejudice to bear and/or prevent us from trying out other ways of seeing or even being.

Because we are so busy acting and reacting, we are not always aware of our constructs, especially the limiting ones, so we may need time to contemplate them or the help of others to explore them and present alternatives. Personal construct theory is an optimistic approach in this respect because it provides tools to help us explore our own constructs and those of others and because it encourages the challenge of constructs which might make us less effective than we might be in a particular situation. The words of eminent practitioners of personal construct theory serve to summarise these last two points. Fransella and Bannister (1989, p. 5) write of the approach being an attempt 'to stand in the other's shoes, to see the world as they see it, to understand their situations, their concerns'.

Kelly (1955, p. 43), the originator of the theory, proposed that 'Since man [*sic*] is always faced with constructive alternatives, which he may explore if he wishes, he need not continue indefinitely to be the absolute victim either of his past history or his present circumstances'.

Chapter 10

The Able Child at Home

There is no doubt that stimulation during the first five years of a child's life is of vital importance. It is during those years that a child learns to talk and to socialise and to respond to various stimuli. We are all aware that the ideal is that they need safety and security and a settled home life that is free from disruption, to enable them to develop as confident people whose aim is to attain their potential. The popular press and books on parentcraft all emphasise the importance of a healthy lifestyle which includes enough sleep, a balanced diet, exercise and socialisation with other children.

Having taken these points into consideration, however, there are certain other aspects which arose from the research and which were particularly commented upon by the parents. They are presented here to act as a guide to parents and to make them aware of possible pitfalls.

Early years

The majority of all the able children in this study, both achievers and under-achievers, had highly developed vocabularies and were able to use language to great effect. For instance, Fergus was able to persuade adults to see his point of view and used this to his advantage. Harriet, Bryony and Cara were all highly skilled at written English and were able to use a number of different styles to suit various audiences. All these children had parents who devoted time and energy to developing their language during the children's early years. Their parents played with them verbally as much as possible, helping them to understand that language games can be fun, for example nursery rhymes, songs, poetry, plays on words and puns. They also helped them to use their imagination in dramatic play and discussed the stories read with them. Further, they were provided with plenty of books and their parents presented good role models, in that they demonstrated to their children just how much enjoyment can be gained from books.

In addition, these children had varied interests outside school including playing numerous musical instruments, sports, astronomy, chess, acting, debating and horse riding, to name but a few. They were taken to many places of interest in order to satisfy their thirst for knowledge and the parents tried to answer their questions to the best of their ability. Jack's parents commented that he was always asking questions, especially when he was younger. Although they tried, there were times when they couldn't answer his questions but, instead of feeling guilty, they made a point of working on the questions together by going to a library or by consulting an encyclopaedia.

In the opinion of a number of parents, it was advisable to encourage children to have varied interests and leisure pursuits, whatever their ability, be it academic, musical or sporting. In their collective opinion, a person who has a wide range of interests is likely to be more fulfilled and to take a broader outlook on life.

Emotional and social development

Parents are best placed to understand a child's emotional difficulties and to help a child to deal with them. Perhaps one of the most important issues is making a child feel good about his/her abilities. The happy and successful achieving children in this study all had high self-esteem. A child with a high self-esteem is more likely to succeed than a child whose opinion of her/himself is low. Having said that, although particular children may be able, few people are good at everything and they shouldn't expect to be. One able child who seemed well adjusted in many respects, refused to take a piano exam because she was worried that she wouldn't get a distinction. This child needed help to understand and to accept her failures, or indeed an ordinary pass grade, as well as her successes. Trying for perfection in everything is seldom a recipe for happiness.

As was seen in the research, some children felt different from other children or were seen as being different by other children, on account of their ability. They were *loners* because they thought they had little in common with their peers. We have already discussed Harriet's problems in this respect, but there were other children with similar problems. Toby felt that his interests rarely coincided with those of his peers and Edward felt the same way. Alistair repeatedly wanted children to do things his way and had not developed the social skills to enable him to listen and to share the opinions of others. He needed to be helped to accept his ability but also to be tolerant of others and to appreciate that others are worth valuing, whatever their talents. In this way his social integration could have been assisted and this in turn could have contributed towards his happiness.

Another problem in this area is that of children hiding their ability in order to gain peer acceptance. Fergus is a prime example of this. He enjoyed being 'one of the lads' so much so that he was willing to sacrifice his academic success for peer acceptance. The boys in this research were more prone to this than girls. An attitude which may be worth adopting is one that stresses the maxim 'It's OK to be bright' and it again may help to reinforce the idea that all people are different and that we should accept them for that. The world would certainly be very boring if we were all the same!

Specific learning difficulties

Our advice to parents would be that if you feel that your child has a specific learning difficulty which has not been identified, then the sooner you seek help and advice, the better. Very often an able child who is having problems with work will be operating at the level of an average child and so his/her ability may be masked. One parent in the study realised that from a teacher's viewpoint, it is not easy to detect such children and thought that patience on her part was very important. She approached the problem by asking advice and trying to be reasonable at all times. She thought it important to remember that her child was one of 30 and there were many demands on the teacher's time. However, the teacher was a sensitive professional and took the time to listen to her problems and to sort them out in the best possible way.

Other problems at school

Children may have other problems at school. For instance there were several children in the study who were poorly motivated or had a short attention span. The children said they were bored at school. This may have been because the tasks set were not challenging enough or it may indeed be due to other causes. In any case, it is always advisable for parents to make an appointment to see their child's teacher as soon as it is recognised that a problem exists, so that it can be talked over and advice sought.

Valuing education

All parents of achievers valued education and their attitudes towards the schools their children attended were, in the main, positive. Some of the parents of the under-achievers also valued education but the children's under-achievement was related to different matters. However, it was felt that under-valuing education could have had a negative influence on their children's achievement patterns. Sarah's mother openly said that she had no interest in knowledge and education whereas others displayed this in their attitude towards the school and in their aspirations for their children.

Knowledge of the education system

The parents of the achievers were well acquainted with just what was going on in schools and how their children were being educated. There are several books generally available which explain the structure of the National Curriculum and the four key stages. In brief a child will be required to sit a test at the end of each key stage, i.e. at 7 years the end of Key Stage 1; at 11 years at the end of Key Stage 2; at 14 years at the end of Key Stage 3; and at 16 years at the end of Key Stage 4 (GCSE).

One teacher in the study felt that teachers at her school were never challenged by the parents or asked to explain why some things were done. She put this down to their lack of knowledge of the education system.

High expectations

There was a striking difference between the expectations of the parents of the achieving children and those of the parents of the under-achieving children. The parents of the achievers expected their children to do well and to go on to higher education whereas the parents of the under-achievers were more likely to have low or indefinite expectations. When asked by the researcher if she wanted her son to go to a university, Rowan's mother considered that although it might be a good idea, it was unlikely because:

we're not a family of scholars, we don't do that sort of thing.

It would be a waste of potential if a child was denied higher education because it wasn't the norm for the family.

Generally the parents of the achievers thought it a good idea to keep options open and to consult teachers and, later on, careers advisers with regards to future alternatives for their children's education.

Undue pressure

One thing that must be guarded against, in the opinion of Eleanor's mother, is that parents' enthusiasm for their child to achieve isn't converted into pressure, as this is sometimes counter-productive (Eleanor was an achiever). Alistair's mother constantly monitored everything her child did in school. This child also had other difficulties but it was felt by the child's teacher that too much pressure was put on the child to achieve and that this contributed to his under-achievement.

Jack's parents wanted him to have the things that were denied them, namely a university education, but in addition to this his father wanted him to become a professional footballer. Perhaps we should beware of living out our ambitions through our children and let them live their own lives, of course with parental guidance and encouragement, as long as ultimately they make decisions for themselves.

Encouraging independence

Independence is probably something which is difficult for all parents to encourage but able children will often be more eager than other children to gain independence and to make decisions for themselves. Owen was given responsibility for planning the route to be taken for a family holiday in Scotland. Toby's interest in cooking resulted in some interesting meals for the family. He insisted that all ingredients had to be just right, no substitutions, and every thing he did in the kitchen was very precise. Cara planned the decor for her bedroom. Perhaps it wasn't quite to her parents' taste but it was her decision and she lived in it.

Avoiding family jealousies

Having an able child can be demanding of time, especially if there are other children to consider. Harriet's brother and sister knew that she had social problems and accepted that extra time had to be spent with her because of this. They had no difficulties in that respect and did not resent the attention which she was granted. Harriet's parents seemed to have handled this situation very well.

Keith's parents overcame a similar dilemma by trying to give all the children in the family special time of their own with them. Each child had different activities which they did with their parents and this helped to overcome sibling rivalry.

Self-help groups

Some parents feel that they don't have the knowledge to help their able children and often feel inadequate. There is no need for despair because help is at hand in the form of the National Association for Gifted Children, a self-help group for parents. At venues all over the country, meetings are held to support parents and their able children. There are also weekend courses for children. (The address is given at the end of the book.)

Sophie's mother felt rather at a loss when her daughter, who started school with a reading age of 7.5, was forced to join the rest of her class to do work which she had already mastered. As a teacher herself she was reluctant to interfere but after three years of seeing her daughter becoming more and more disenchanted with school life and indeed developing behavioural problems, she thought it was time that she acted. She had read about the NAGC and sought their advice. They recommended that she should look for a school which would encourage her daughter's ability and not try to demean it.

Sophie was sent to a school where her ability was not looked upon as being mere precocity. At the end of only one term in her new school, she was thriving in every respect. In fact she became a much happier child and was easier to deal with. Her mother attributes this to the fact that she was praised for her ability and academic success and consequently her self-esteem improved.

Good parent–teacher rapport

Good parent–teacher relationships seemed to be linked with achievement in the study. It is clearly worthwhile for parents to try to manage relationships with the school well. Some parents in the research felt embarrassed to talk to the teacher about their child's ability because they didn't like to boast. This was a common feeling amongst the parents and one parent who also happened to be a teacher remarked that:

> all children are entitled to education which will help them to reach their potential and any teacher worth their salt will know the ability of the children in their class quite quickly, so talking about the child shouldn't be a problem.

Another parent felt that the way to proceed was to ask the teacher's impressions of the child first to provide a basis from which to start.

Generally it was felt that being supportive of the school meant attending meetings, fund-raising and social activities and helping in any other way possible. Being supportive of your child meant helping to provide books for particular projects and making sure that assignments were completed on time. A parent who had herself experienced emotional difficulties believed that problems at home which are likely to affect a child's work should be discussed with the child's teacher without delay. The teacher can then support the child to the best of his/her ability.

Having taken all these points into consideration, the next important step for parents is to choose a school for their child.

Choosing a school

As has been reiterated throughout this book, able children need challenge in their education. When selecting a school there are some attributes which the parent of an able child may want to consider. The first is whether a policy for able children exists in the school and, if so, whether there is a particular member of staff responsible for monitoring the progress of able children. Other points are whether children are placed in sets according to ability for particular subjects, whether the opportunities for able children to work together at times exists and what particular extra-curricular clubs are provided.

When visiting a school one is usually able to gauge the atmosphere of the place and it is important to find out whether the school would suit a particular child. Is he or she more suited to formality or informality, to order or to a more relaxed atmosphere? Another area which is worth consideration is how welcome are parents. Are any parents visible, maybe helping in the classrooms, during visits? How often are parents invited to the school to visit their child's teacher or for other reasons, for instance workshop sessions on maths or reading schemes used in the school. This is an important issue for parents who feel that they would like to be closely involved with their child's education.

Inevitably parents will be asked to present their view of their child. They shouldn't feel embarrassed to discuss what they have observed about their child's development. A diary/scrapbook recording milestones of development may be useful at this point. They may feel that they would like to comment on some of the following points:

- Early development – at what age the child walked and talked.
- Early learning ability, e.g. reading.
- Vocabulary- is the child's vocabulary considered to be extensive for his/her age?
- Their personality – sociable, quiet? What is the parental estimation of their self-esteem?
- Interests.
- Concentration and attention skills – is he/she able to stick at something for a length of time?
- Memory – are there any instances which surprised parents about the child's memory?
- Imagination – did he/she indulge in dramatic play at an early age? Does he/she like to write stories or poetry?
- Artistic ability – is he/she artistic? Perhaps he/she has a modelling ability, e.g. using Lego.
- Ability to socialise – is he/she a loner or does he/she find it easy to socialise?
- What can parents say about his/her powers of observation?
- Is he/she curious?
- What can parents say about his/her reasoning powers?

After making the initial contact with the school, parents may want to make a further appointment once the child has been in the school for a few weeks. This will have given the child's teacher time to assess him/her and parents will then be able to discuss the child and the way he or she has settled.

In conclusion

To sum up, all the points mentioned above are worthy of consideration if the goal is that children should develop into well-adjusted adults whose potential has been fulfilled. A consideration is that academic ability is not the only thing to bear in mind when thinking of a child's education. A child's emotional and social development, plus encouraging a wide variety of interests, are also important.

If a child sees that parents value education and that they have some knowledge of the system, then he or she is likely to look on it favourably. High expectations are commendable as long as they are realistic and don't become off-putting for the child.

Lastly, choose a child's school with care, ascertaining if a particular school is right for him/her. It is worthwhile working at maintaining a close relationship with a child's teacher and school. Then, if problems do arise, parents may not feel reluctant to share them, as a number of parents in this study reported. It is as well to remember that the earlier difficulties are dealt with, the better.

The next chapter seeks to present an overview of the book, commenting on the results and suggestions previously made.

Chapter 11

Final Words

In previous chapters we have introduced you to some people we got to know well in the course of our research: teachers, parents and able children, achievers and under-achievers. None of these were paragons of virtue. Like all of us they were struggling to conduct their lives as best they knew how in diverse and often difficult circumstances. In Chapter 2 the literature and theories about intelligence were detailed, and in Chapter 3 we set the national scene which formed the background to these lives. In subsequent chapters more details were provided about particular school and family situations and personal responses to them. In this chapter we will draw these threads together, providing a general overview of results and suggestions deriving from our work, paying attention to the people involved in the situation, firstly from our perspective and lastly presenting their viewpoints.

Teachers

During the time the research took place, teachers were beset by problems related to a number of factors, firstly that of the national context. At that time the British education system was undergoing a series of changes. The implementation of the National Curriculum meant that teachers were inundated with a great deal of paperwork related to assessment procedures and they had to deal with yet a further change when the Dearing modifications to the National Curriculum were implemented in January 1994. So the 1990s saw the initiation of a great period of change for all those involved in the education profession.

With regard to the particular schools involved in this research, the location and catchment area of all three schools was different as were the attitudes and achievement patterns of the pupils. One was predominantly middle class and parental expectations were very high. These parents were vociferous in their criticism of teachers if the need arose. The second was a mixture of middle- and working-class parents so that resources that children had access to outside school ranged widely, and the third was predominantly working class. In this third school the parents rarely criticised the teachers, a situation which was thought by one of the staff to be unhealthy.

Resources in all three schools, with regard to children of all abilities, seemed good, but perhaps the school in the middle-class area was slightly better equipped because it had a very supportive parent–teacher association.

For all three schools, at the time the research took place, their support from their local authorities with regard to courses on and advice about able children was scanty. In fact none of the teachers who took part in this research had been on a course which was specifically designed to help teachers meet the needs of their more able pupils. Fortunately, the situation has now changed in that a number of counties have produced guidelines for teachers on how to make provision for able children, and most run courses on this subject.

In all schools included in this study, the children were taught in mixed-ability classes. Of course this has social advantages in that children are free to mix with others who have a variety of talents, but it does have some educational drawbacks. As one of the parents, who also happened to be a teacher, stated, mixed-ability teaching often means that teachers are so busy dealing with the needs of the slow-learning children that little time is left for the able. When considering the busy life of a class teacher this attitude is easy to understand, but it does nothing to help the able child. One answer could be the practice of setting for core subjects but, again, this only deals with a fraction of the time a child spends in school. Individual differentiation for children who need this could be another response while acceleration for a particular subject, such as educating a Year 4 child for maths with Year 6 children, may be a third strategy for helping a teacher to cope with the demands of the able.

Parents

Parents too had to cope with problems related to a range of factors. Economically speaking the south of England is an expensive area in which to live with regard to housing and has possibly a higher cost of living index compared with other regions. To compound this some parents may have to contend with redundancy and the subsequent hardships which accompany it.

Partnership problems was another factor which many parents had to cope with. A large percentage of the under-achieving children in this study had parents who were divorced or separated. Although marital breakdown is not uncommon, the emotional effect that this has on a child must not be under-estimated. Also, the amount of time which a parent has to spend with a child and their commitment to family life is often reduced when a divorce or separation occurs. As previously discussed, McLanaghan (1992) indicated that there is no definite proof that divorce itself causes lower attainment, but perhaps because a single parent has more commitments, the attention a child receives may be less than before the family breakdown.

However, even when a child does live with just one parent only, if that child receives support for his/her education and lives in a stable home environment, then he/she may still achieve. One point which must be considered is that some children may be happier overall after divorce or separation has occurred because there is no longer continuous discord in the family. Such an improvement in their environment may therefore facilitate achievement (Weisner and Garnier, 1992).

Having an able child in the family may bring difficulties, as described in Chapter 10, especially when there are other children to consider within the family setting. The avoidance of sibling jealousies is certainly not easy but might be partially achieved if parents set aside time to spend specifically with other members of the family so that the able child is not always the centre of attention.

Able children do sometimes behave in a problematic way. As has been discussed earlier, some like Harriet have social problems. Perhaps one way to overcome this is to encourage tolerance of others. In contrast, others, like Fergus, hide their abilities for peer acceptance. They need to realise that it is 'OK to be bright'.

Another complication which sometimes arises is that of children asking questions about topics and issues which are beyond their parents' knowledge. As parents ourselves of able children, we have frequently been in that unenviable position! It is no disgrace to admit to 'not knowing' and to search out the required information together.

Children

The children in the study were themselves having to deal with a complex array of constraints and opportunities. For instance they were often bored at school because at times they found the work unchallenging. For greater consistency their needs have to be considered at the planning stage so that work given when they have finished a particular task does not become a 'bolted-on extra' intended just to keep them occupied. Such advance planning helps to ensure that the child will remain motivated.

Able children should also be allowed to work together for part of the time so that they can be stimulated by 'bouncing ideas' off each other. Although the climate seems to be changing, there was a time when the education of able children was thought to be elitist and, for egalitarian reasons, their needs were sidelined. As teachers we are all aware of the times when during class discussions we have thought to ourselves 'no I can't let him/her answer yet again', but perhaps for that child's self-esteem and to help develop a sense of fair play, it might be reasonable to explain our actions.

As we have seen, many able children feel isolated by their difference from their peers. To isolate them also from adult approval only adds to the problem. Loneliness to a child is a high price to pay for intellectual advancement.

At this juncture we would like to give the participants their final say. All these comments arose from interviews and are presented in diagrammatic form together with a summary of their comments.

The parents

The parents of achieving children (see Figure 11.1) seemed not discontented with the education their children were receiving. Most of them thought that their children were being extended academically, although they did have reservations. They thought that specialist teachers, trained to enrich the curriculum of able children, would be highly beneficial. It appears from their perspective, though, that little will be done about this until teachers understand the plight of the able child and are willing and able to make it a priority.

Another criticism was that the children did not have enough time to follow their particular interests. However, on this point, it would be correct to make a case on the teachers' behalf. Although the National Curriculum was slimmed down in 1994, time constraints were such that little time was left for anything not already on the curriculum. As parents ourselves, and busy ones at that, we are only too well aware that we should not abdicate our responsibilities to teachers. There are many activities and interests which can be pursued in hometime and require some parental support.

A third major criticism was lack of appropriate work. Throughout the research there was evidence of differentiation occurring in schools. Usually this consisted of tasks being set at differing levels per child for core subjects, usually just English and mathematics. What was noticeable, however, was that there was little individual differentiation in type of task. Often the children were given a similar exercise to complete when they had finished a piece of work and this led to repetition and boredom.

In their parents' eyes, the majority of these children were confident and had a high self-esteem. They were well motivated had few social problems (although some parents described their children as 'loners') and enjoyed competition. These parents had positive aspirations for their children and expected them to do well. It was evident that they valued education, supported school activities and were very interested in their children's progress.

Figure 11.1 shows in summary the attributes which were considered by the parents of the achieving children to lead to achievement. Factors which were commonly mentioned, but were not necessarily linked to achievement, are shown without arrows.

One of the main differences between the parents of the achievers and the parents of the under-achievers (see Figure 11.2) was that the parents of the latter talked of, or at least intimated, the lack of cooperation between them and the school. For a child to succeed, close cooperation between parents and teachers is at least

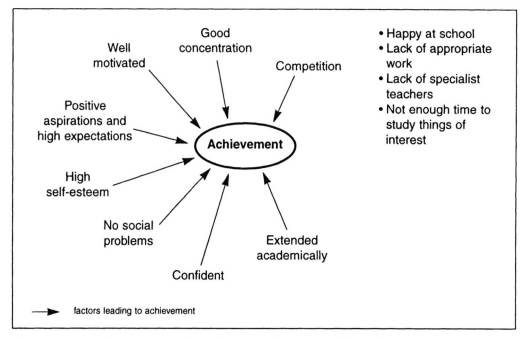

Figure 11.1   Themes related to achievement from parents' interviews

desirable if not essential.

A great many of these children had emotional problems, often connected with an unstable home background and marital breakdown. As has already been discussed, family discord has been linked with under-achievement in several studies. Other children had emotional problems which may be related to or exacerbated by the parents exerting too much pressure on them to achieve.

Some of the children who came from families where marital relations had broken down exhibited financial deprivation. Financial insecurity and the limitations it places upon a family have been observed to have detrimental effects upon achievement patterns (Hitchfield, 1973; Smilansky and Nevo, 1979; Freeman, 1991). This may lead to a child's ability not being recognised.

Some parents felt that the school should do more to tackle lack of motivation and low self-esteem in particular. Several parents felt that they could do little to help their child with their school work, either because they were reluctant to interfere or because they were not competent to do so. In many cases this was not stated explicitly but was inferred. This insecurity about their own role or competence did not apply to all parents of under-achieving children, however. Eleven out of the sixteen under-achievers did, though, have parents who were not supportive for one reason or another.

Like the parents of the achieving children, the parents of the under-achievers criticised the lack of specialist help given to their children and the inappropriate work they were sometimes given. Since the children in this study were very able, the attainment level of an under-achieving child was often on a par with that of a child of average ability. This resulted in them not being seen as seriously under-achieving and hence they did not merit additional assistance. It was reported by some parents that their children were subjected to peer group pressure and apparently, for this reason, deliberately under-achieved in order not to appear different from the majority.

These parents had no definite aspirations or expectations for their children and this stood out in sharp contrast to the parents of the achievers. In some cases this was because they had no experience of higher education, describing their family as not being a family of scholars; in other cases they did not value education; and finally, some had become discouraged by their child's problems and lack of achievement.

Figure 11.2 displays in summary the opinions of the parents of the under-achieving children. The one factor not associated with under-achievement is shown without an arrow.

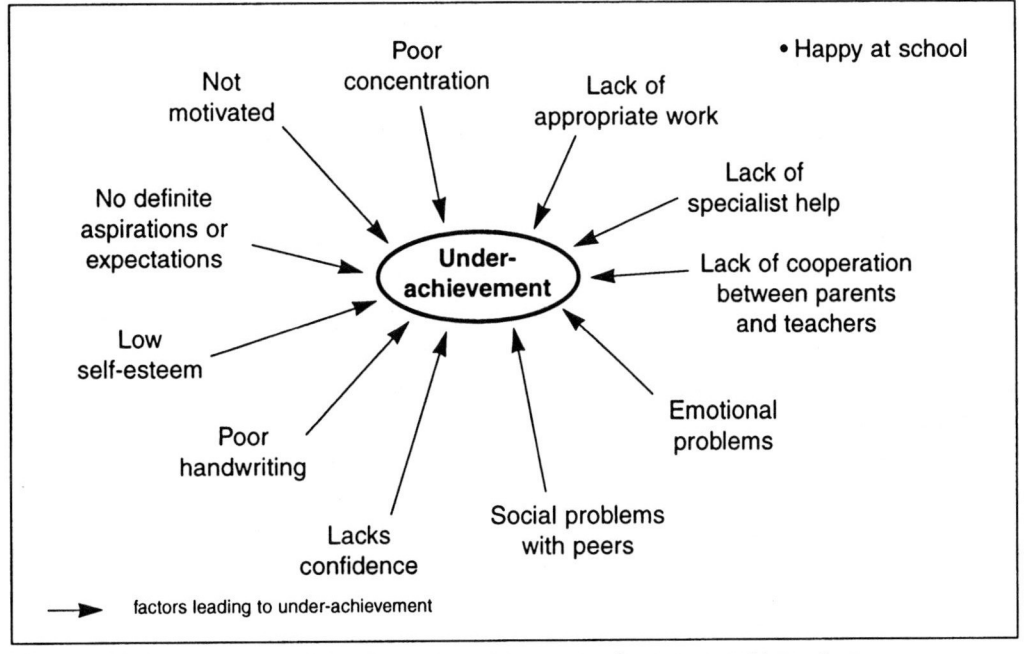

Figure 11.2 Themes related to under-achievement from parents' interviews

Teachers

For achievement to occur, the teachers saw a good rapport between the child and the teacher to be of the utmost importance. If the children have this support, then the teacher was able to motivate, bolster self-esteem, and encourage independence while at the same time being sympathetic to the child's needs. Teachers also felt that they should be flexible and versatile, and should help the child to think laterally. They were aware that a teacher should set tasks that were at an appropriate level for the children in order to challenge them and to extend their capabilities. In their opinion, a good teacher should also be able to spot ability. This was what they thought of as encompassing teacher support. These teachers had high expectations of their achieving pupils and this hopefully affected the children in a positive manner.

A partnership between teacher and parent was thought to be essential if the child was to reach his/her potential. Parents were thought to be supportive if they encouraged aspects of school work, valued education, had high but realistic expectations and had a sound knowledge of the education system.

An important aspect concerning the child was thought to be a match between intellectual abilities and the ability to channel this intelligence. It was thought to be embodied in combinations of the following: rapid assimilation of new concepts; being anxious to please; a high level of research skills; confidence and an eagerness to achieve; a high standard of work and presentation; a well adjusted personality; high self-esteem; and lastly, a good attention span and work ethic.

Attributes such as an eagerness to please and a well adjusted personality point to conformity as being a contributory factor to success. This could indeed be the case for it is unusual to succeed in any system with which one is at odds. At least it takes a very strong, confident personality, in addition to being very talented, to do so. Stimulation gained from the children working with others of a similar ability was thought desirable but not always possible within one class. For this to be possible, it would involve organising children from different classes to work together. Teachers did recognise an *ideal* situation in the school which would be conducive to the development of potential, but acknowledged the limits that practicality places on this in the current educational/economic climate.

Figure 11.3 summarises the opinions of the teachers of achieving children and encapsulates their view of parental and teacher support, as well their conception of the achieving child. Lack of specialist teachers was a topic which was frequently commented upon, and is shown without an arrow.

The problems of the under-achiever were seen as three-fold:

1. *The child.* Generally the child's problems were viewed as a mismatch in intellectual abilities and the ability to channel their intelligence. The specific problems were as follows: seeks adult attention all the time; low self-esteem; an inability to see him/herself as an achiever; lack of concentration; poor handwriting and presentation; an inability to apply him/herself; lack of perseverance; poor social skills; no self-discipline; insecurity and emotional disturbance.

   An under-achieving child could manifest all these problems or a selection of them. However, all were seen as factors linked to under-achievement.

2. *The parents.* In the teachers' eyes, lack of parental support was a major contributory factor leading to under-achievement. A number of parents of under-achievers were thought to be unsupportive of their children in one respect or another. However, support had to be of the right kind. Too much pressure on a child to achieve was seen as being detrimental and therefore unsupportive. At the other extreme was the parent who did not value education and therefore was not interested in a child's progress at school. Some parents were reported as talking negatively about the schools and this filtered through to the children. It was felt that this was very damaging for the child.

3. *The school.* One problem was low teacher expectations. It was evident that some teachers thought that the difficulties experienced by some children were so great that they would be hard to overcome. These anxieties were voiced during the interviews. It is not surprising that children were not encouraged by such low expectations of them.

There were also problems associated with mixed-ability teaching. Several teachers were concerned that they had little time to spend with able children, as the less able children were so demanding and took up a disproportionate amount of time. Equally a lack of specialist teachers did not help, i.e. teachers particularly trained to deal with the needs of able children. All teachers would have welcomed some additional support. If more were available, then at least some of these problems could have been reduced.

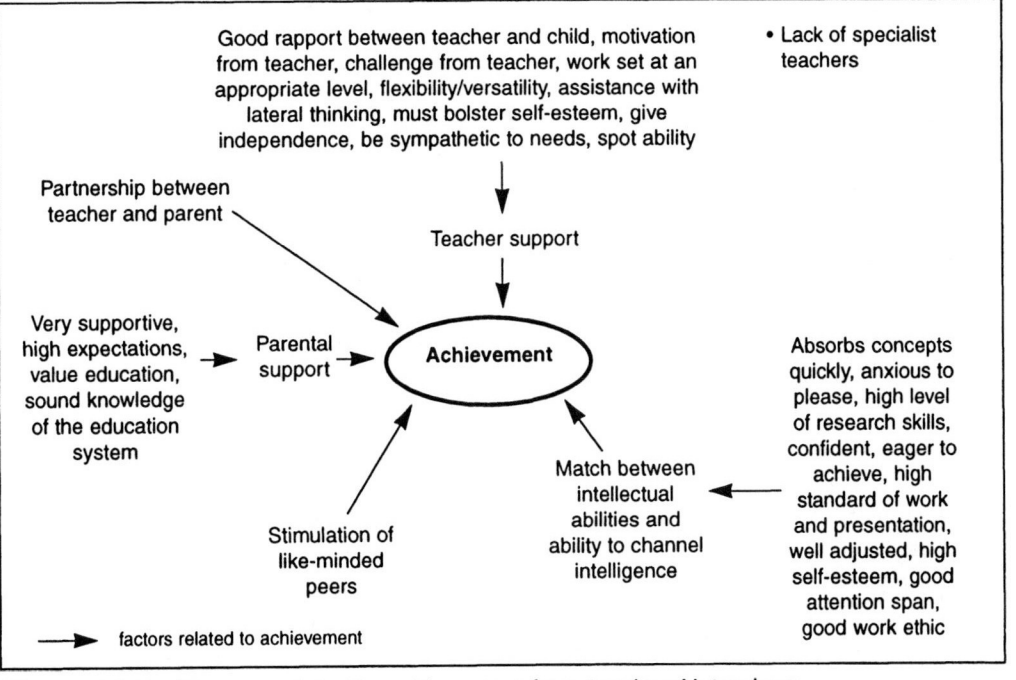

Figure 11.3 Themes related to achievement from teachers' interviews

Figure 11.4 outlines the major factors which the teachers felt were associated with under-achievement. The item shown without the arrow (children liking school) was not thought by the researcher to be linked to under-achievement but is included since most teachers felt that children liked school although they were not achieving their potential.

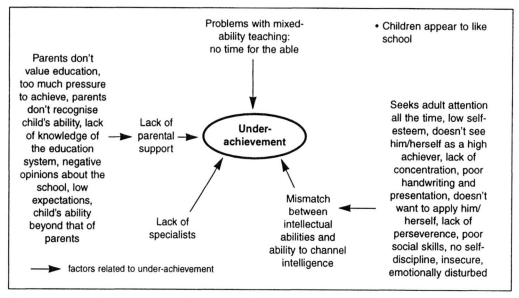

Figure 11.4   Themes related to under-achievement from teachers' interviews

Two-thirds of all these children, both achievers and under-achievers, were thought by their teachers to exhibit creativity. This took a variety of forms, for example, Harriet's creativity lay in the realm of writing and the same may be said of Eleanor and Bryony, all achievers; Fergus, an under-achiever was outstandingly talented with all aspects of drama and was also considered to have particular mathematical talent; Toby was an excellent musician, as was Jane, both under-achievers; Jack, apart from achieving in most aspects of the curriculum, was a notable athlete; Jay, an achiever, had a particular flair for mathematics and Alexander, an under-achiever, had artistic talent.

Children

The majority of the achieving children thought themselves to be good all-rounders. The list of interests each produced demonstrated that they enjoyed a variety of activities. They reported that they were happy at school and all except one related that they had no social difficulties. They made it clear that they liked work which required thought but disliked repetition or tasks which they thought too easy. The majority thought that their handwriting was well formed and their presentation good. To them, a good teacher was one who was helpful, had a sense of humour, took a personal interest in them, was fair, enthusiastic, kind and exciting. This person should not be strict but at the same time should make the children work 'properly'.

Figure 11.5 encapsulates the opinions of the achieving children. Topics shown without arrows were frequently mentioned by the children. They were not connected with achievement but were difficulties which they perceived as existing though they had overcome them.

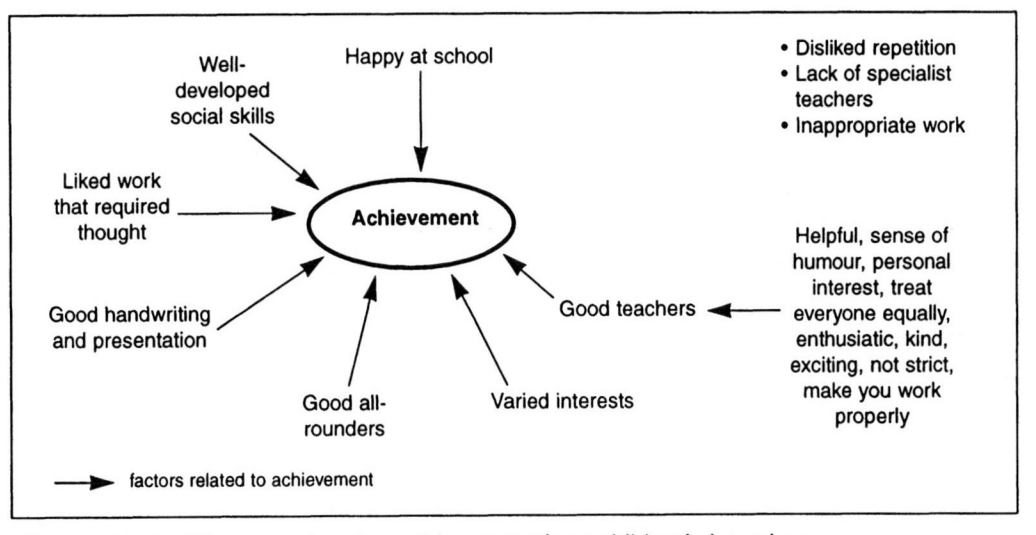

Figure 11.5 Themes related to achievement from children's interviews

Like the achieving children, the under-achievers were reportedly happy at school. The children themselves, however, were not quite so definite or convinced on this point as their parents and teachers. They tended to think that some elements of school were acceptable, but the enthusiasm which the parents and teachers reported was not evident.

Many of them seemed incapable of forming lasting relationships with their peers and reported feeling unhappy because of this. Their interests, however, from the lists related, were as varied as those of the achieving children. Perhaps one of the greatest differences, though, was that most of them had poorly developed skills of concentration and non-fluent handwriting. They reported that they often had to repeat written work because their handwriting was poor and they found that repetition tedious.

Their idea of a good teacher was similar to that of the achievers. In addition, they required a good teacher to be informal, not dominant, amusing, flexible, even tempered and not annoying. Also, this person should be able to recognise ability.

Figure 11.6 summarises the opinions of the under-achieving children. Topics shown without arrows are not associated with under-achievement, but describe attributes common to the under-achieving children.

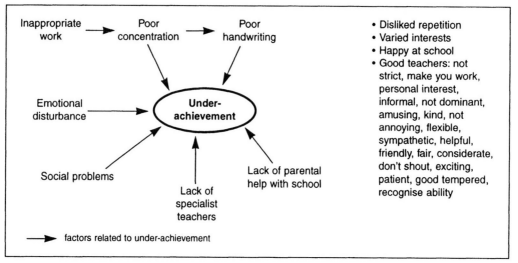

Figure 11.6   Themes related to under-achievement from children's interviews

A way forward

This research has made us appreciate that under-achieving children are difficult to identify. A teacher has to be very sensitive to the way children handle language, assimilate new ideas and concepts and to their individual approach to problem solving. If a child displays talent in just one respect but is not an achiever, then he/she is worthy of further investigation.

Standardised tests can help to identify such children, especially those who hide their ability deliberately for peer group acceptance. However, tests do have their limitations in that they can be culturally biased and must therefore be chosen carefully; also one must appreciate that a test is one measurement taken at one particular time under a particular set of circumstances. Observation which takes place over time can be more informative and accurate. Perhaps a combination of both methods would be the better option.

This study has displayed to us that not all children are treated equally with regard to school resources. A school should cater fairly for the educational needs of all its pupils. The argument that able children will survive unaided because of their ability is flawed. They need education which includes a high level of challenge. Without recognition of their ability and a programme which is designed particularly to meet their needs, not only will they not reach their potential, but they may accumulate other difficulties. A child subjected to inappropriate education may become disaffected; this in turn may link with difficulties with relationships or other behavioural problems.

To conclude we would like to recognise here that able children can be difficult to teach and also difficult to live with but we would also like to call for flexibility on behalf of all those involved in the care and education of able children. Perhaps it is as well to recognise that we are all complex creatures and that what suits one does not suit all. We all have different motives, priorities and resources. Therefore we need to tailor our skills, and the resources we have available, to the context, but most importantly to the needs of the children in our care.

A greater awareness of the importance of the child's perspective has been appreciated during the course of this research. This has added a significant dimension which, in the past, has been sorely neglected. Perhaps, as teachers and parents, we should listen more to the views and opinions of our pupils/children.

The following extract supports our feelings on listening to and observing children. It also illustrates a warning to teachers and parents to ignore to their detriment, the little treasures children show them.

Poem for Everyman

I will present you
parts
of
my
self
slowly
if you are patient and tender.
I will open drawers
that stay mostly closed
and bring out places and people and things
sounds and smells, loves and frustrations, hopes and sadnesses ...
altogether – you or i will never see them –
they are me.
If you regard them lightly
deny they are important
or worse, judge them
i will quietly, slowly
begin to wrap them up
in small pieces of velvet,
like worn silver and gold jewellery,
tuck them away
in a small wooden chest of drawers

and close.

(Wood, 1983)

Appendix A: Enrichment Materials

The following associations produce published materials suitable for primary-aged children and may be contacted at the following addresses.

National Association for Able Children in Education
Westminster College
Oxford OX2 9AT

National Association for Gifted Children
Elder House
Milton Keynes MK9 ILR

Ongar Curriculum Support Centre
Fyfield Road
Chipping Ongar
Essex CM5 0AL

Able Children (Pullen Publications) Ltd
13 Station Road
Knebworth
Herts SG3 6AP

GIFT Ltd
5 Ditton Court Road
Westcliff-on-Sea
Essex SO0 7HG

Appendix B: Pupil–Teacher Interactions Militating Against Pupil Achievement

Failing to take a personal interest in the child

a) The teacher becoming irritated by constant questioning, not answering these questions and not giving the child the opportunity to find the answers for him/herself.

Example 1: Charles was constantly asking questions. He had a wide general knowledge and was eager to acquire more. They were discussing sound and his question concerned the Doppler Effect. Possibly his teacher could not explain this (this is not a criticism as his teacher was not a science specialist) and she reminded him that he was not the only person in the class and that he should give other children the chance to ask questions. Charles seemed to resent this. The child could have been presented with a challenge to find the answer to the question himself and then this could have been presented to the class.

Example 2: Harriet and her teacher were often at odds and this became apparent during periods when the teacher was discussing topics with the class. On this particular occasion the teacher was talking about right angles. Harriet wanted to know why it was called a right angle and not a left angle but failed to get an answer. Again, this could have been turned into an opportunity for the child to find out the information for herself.

Example 3: Karl needed constant reassurance about his work. He was meticulous and worked slowly. On one particular occasion his teacher told him, sternly, to sit down and to get on with his work and to stop asking questions. While sympathising with the teacher, (she had a large class and many things to do), this could have been done in a more sensitive manner. The child was unnecessarily upset.

b) Allowing other children to interrupt while talking to the child.

Example 1: James needed help with a mathematics problem and had at last got the attention of the teacher. He did not get the time that he needed for the explanation of the problem because the teacher allowed herself to be dragged away by the demands of other children. Consequently he lost interest in his work and started to disturb other children around him.

Example 2: Freya wanted her teacher to check through her topic work so that she could progress to the next stage. She managed to talk to her teacher for a very short time only and then he started to deal with another child who was misbehaving and Freya did not get any more teacher attention that lesson.

Example 3: While talking over a problem-solving exercise that Alexander was involved with, the teacher never gave him her full attention. She was constantly issuing instructions to other children and answering other queries.

c) Allowing little time for able children to talk over problems.

Example 1: After the introduction to the lesson which concerned materials and their properties, the teacher gave out worksheets (differentiated) but failed to give any explanation to the more able. They were expected to read the worksheet and start. Ralph became rather frustrated at the lack of teacher intervention. He did understand what was required of him and it was really a matter of reassuring him that he was on the right track. With a little help from the researcher he was able to start.

Example 2: Mark had been sitting puzzling over a piece of work on scientific discoveries in Victorian times. He had been unable to attract the teacher's attention and when at last he was noticed, the amount of teacher time he received was negligible. This resulted in the child feeling very frustrated, shown by his resigned look and the conversation which he started with the child sitting beside him.

Example 3: Saskia would often sit doing nothing for a long periods of time whenever she was asked to do a piece of written work. This often resulted in the child becoming disruptive and disturbing other children. If more teacher time had been given to her, or even time with a classroom assistant, then this situation could possibly have been avoided.

d) Teacher becoming annoyed at a child's lack of application without finding out the reason for this (possibly as a result of absence of teacher attention).

Example 1: Keith had been told to work on a mathematics exercise concerning time which was similar to the one he had completed. He had no problem in understanding the work set but it appeared not to challenge him. He became distracted and spent a long time sharpening his pencil. Eventually the teacher became annoyed and told him to get on with his work.

Example 2: Toby was often distracted. It seemed that the work set him offered little challenge, together with the fact that he received little teacher time. On numerous occasions he was spoken to sharply because he often wandered around the room talking to other children. More demanding tasks and more teacher time could possibly have altered the situation.

Example 3: Sarah was easily distracted but on one particular occasion she had been upset by an incident which had happened at playtime. Her relationships with her peers was not an easy one. On returning to the classroom she sat and did nothing. At this her teacher became very annoyed and told her that she would be sent to the headteacher if she did not get on with her work. It was not until the researcher had time to speak to her later on that morning that she was told about her upsetting experience at playtime. Her teacher was informed of this at lunch time.

e) Low teacher expectations.

Example 1: Charles had given a piece of topic work to his teacher. It was not well presented and she became irritated. She commented that that was all she could really expect from him and asked him to repeat it neatly.

Example 2: On finding that Fergus had not started a piece of work his teacher told him that he wasn't surprised, it was what he expected.

Example 3: On inspecting a piece of English work that Anthony had completed his teacher reacted in a negative manner. It was not what she actually said but the way she commented. This appeared very off-hand and must have made the child feel under-valued. He did find handwriting difficult and any piece of work which was actually finished should have been a triumph.

f) Negative comments when annoyed with the child.

The last set of examples covered negative comments as well as low teacher expectations. These comments also exemplify the former.

Example 1: James was an anxious child who worked very slowly. Often he seemed unwilling to ask for help when it was required. On one occasion he was told to stop day-dreaming and to get on with his work. There was probably a reason why he was not applying himself, but his teacher did not bother to find out why.

Example 2: Freya was talking to other children when she should have been working. However, she had finished her task. She was told that she was always causing a disturbance and was moved to a table by herself.

Example 3: Rowan was another child who was anxious and needed constant reassurance. He did ask for a lot of teacher attention but was told sharply on one occasion to sit down and to get on with his work. I can appreciate that the teacher was overworked and that many children were making demands on her. However, the child was very sensitive and I feel that this could have been handled more delicately.

g) Child not given time to think.

If the child is not writing, he/she may be accused of having their minds on other things.

On numerous occasions children from all three schools were accused of wasting time and day-dreaming. In these cases the children were thinking about what they should write because after the lesson they were asked why they had not been working. Karl commented on this during an interview.

Failing to cater for the needs of the able child

a) Inappropriate work, lacking challenge.

Example 1: Charles gave the impression that he was bored with the English exercise he had been given to do. This concerned putting speech marks in the appropriate places on a given text. His attention span was often not that which the teacher required and during interviews with him, he complained that the work was too easy. On this occasion he talked to other children and then wandered around the room.

Example 2: Toby was an able mathematician and was set a page of arithmetic (division) which, although the work had been differentiated and his task was the most advanced, appeared too easy for him. Consequently he started to 'help' others. This was seen by the teacher as being disruptive.

Example 3: The class had been told a part of the story of Moses during an RE lesson. The task set was for them to retell the story. Although Amelia did finish this quickly, it presented little challenge to her. It appeared that she wanted to get the piece of work finished as quickly as possible so that she would be able to start something else.

b) Repetitive work i.e. giving a child work of a similar nature to that just completed.

Example 1: On one occasion Jay, an able mathematician, having finished the work on data handling she had been set was asked to construct and interpret a similar graph. This task was no more complicated than the last and presented no challenge to her.

Example 2: Both Harriet and Fergus deliberately worked slowly during mathematics and some English lessons (particularly those concerning punctuation and points of grammar). Their reasons for this were that they would be given more work of the same sort. This had been observed on numerous occasions.

Example 3: On one occasion Jack had been asked to do another English exercise similar to the one he had completed. He had finished very quickly, possibly because the exercise did not challenge him enough. He did voice his dismay at being asked to do this and suggested that he did topic work instead. This was denied him.

c) No work planned for able children when set tasks are finished.

Example 1: On one occasion, having finished his topic work ahead of the others, Keith was asked to tidy a bookshelf. On questioning the child about this, he seemed quite happy with the situation and said that this happened quite frequently.

Example 2: On finishing English work early, Zara was asked to write a story of her choice. There was no input from the teacher on this and it appeared to be a ploy to keep the child occupied.

Example 3: Of the three schools included in this study, one concentrated most on art and presentation. Wall displays and topic books were very impressive. However, on numerous occasions, when the children had finished set tasks, they were left to such activities as colouring borders of topic books during prime learning time.

d) Teacher being over critical of handwriting and general presentation and asking the child to repeat work.

Example 1: Charles was often told to repeat work because it was poorly presented. This made for an uneasy relationship between child and teacher. Charles really resented having to do this. The teacher often reported to me that he made little effort.

Example 2: Being told so often that their work was not presentable made both Fergus and Toby feel that the content of their written work was not up to standard. They grew to dislike English in particular and written work in general because they had to repeat it so often. Both children were highly articulate and possessed wide-ranging vocabularies.

e) Instructions not clearly conveyed to the children.

On several occasions, the able children in some classes were given worksheets and told to get on with their work without being given verbal explanations. These instructions were not always explicit. This emphasises the need for teachers to talk to particular groups of children before expecting them to embark on tasks.

Bibliography

Ayles, R. (1991) 'Gifted girls: a case of wasted talent?', in Monks F. J., Katzo M. W., van Boxtel H. W. (eds) *Education of the Gifted in Europe: Theoretical and Research Issues*, 157–61. Amsterdam: Swets & Zeitlinger.

Benn, C. (1982) 'The myth of giftedness, part 2', *Forum* 24, 78–84.

Bloom, B. S. (ed.) (1985) *Developing Talent in Young People*. New York: Ballantine Books.

Colangelo, N., Dettman, D. F. (1983) 'A review of research on parents and families of gifted children', *Exceptional Children* 50, 20–7.

Congdon, P. (1995) 'The gifted, the dyslexic and the left-handed', *Looking to their Future: The Journal of the National Association for Gifted Children*, Spring, 4.

Covington, M. V. (1984) 'The self-worth theory of achievement motivation: findings and implications', *Elementary School Journal* 5, 5–20.

Dalton, P., Dunnett, G. (1992) *A Psychology for Living*. Chichester: Wiley.

DeHaan, R., Havighurst, R. (1957) *Educating Gifted Children*. Chicago, IL: University of Chicago Press.

Department for Education (1992) *Choice and Diversity: A New Framework for Schools*. London: HMSO.

Department for Education (1995) *Key Stages 1 and 2 of the National Curriculum*. London: HMSO.

Douglas, J. (1969) *The Home and the School*. London: MacGibbon and Kee.

Dunn, L. M., Dunn, L. M., Whetton, C., Pintilie, D. (1982) *British Picture Vocabulary Scale*. London: NFER Nelson.

Dunnicliffe, N. (ed.) (1993) *Head Teachers' Legal Guide*. Kingston upon Thames: Cromer Publications.

Emerick, L. J. (1992) 'Academic under achievement among the gifted. Students' perceptions of factors that reverse the pattern', *Gifted Child Quarterly* 36(3), 140–46.

Eyre, D. (1997) *Able Children in Ordinary Schools*. London: David Fulton Publishers.

Eyre, D., Fuller, M. (1993) *Year Six Teachers and More Able Pupils: A Look at the Issues in Providing Appropriate Challenge in the Nine National Curriculum Subject Areas*. National Primary Centre, Oxfordshire County Council.

Eyre, D., Marjoram, T. (1990) *Enriching and Extending the National Curriculum*. London: Kogan Page.

Feldhusen, J., Jarwan, F. (1993) 'Identification of gifted and talented youth for educational programs', in Heller, K., Monks, F., Passow, A. (eds) *International Handbook of Research and Development of Giftedness and Talent*, 233–51. Oxford: Pergamon Press.

Felouzis, G. (1993) 'Class interaction and success at school', *Revue Francais de Sociologie* 34(2), 199–222.

Ferguson, D. M., Lynskey, M. T., Horwood, L. J. (1994) 'The effects of parental separation, the timing of separation and gender on children's performance in cognitive tests', *Journal of child psychology and psychiatry* 35(6), 1077–92.

Fine, M. J., Pitts, R. (1980) 'Intervention and under achieving gifted children: rationale and strategies', *Gifted Child Quarterly* 24(2), 51–5.

Firth, J. (1974) 'The effects of turbulence: the evidence', *RAF Quarterly*, Spring, 19–22.

Flynn, J. M., Rahbar, M. H. (1994) 'Prevalence of reading failure in boys compared with girls', *Psychology in the Schools* 31(1), 66–71.

Fransella, F., Bannister, D. (1989) *A Manual for Repertory Grid Techniques*. London: Academic Press.

Freeman, J. (1979) *Gifted Children*. London: Mather Bros (Printers).

Freeman, J. (1991) *Gifted Children Growing Up*. London: Cassell.

Freeman, J. (1993) 'Parents and families in nurturing giftedness and talent', in Heller, K., Monks, F., Passow, A. (eds) *International Handbook of Research and Development of Giftedness and Talent*, 669–83. Oxford: Pergamon Press.

Freeman, J. (1995) 'Towards a policy for actualizing talent', in Freeman, J., Span, P., Wagner, H. (eds) *Actualizing Talent: A Life-long Challenge?* London: Cassell.

Gagné, F. (1991) 'Towards a differentiated model of giftedness and talent', in Colangelo, N., Davies, G. A. (eds) *Handbook of Gifted Education*, 65–80.

Galton, F. (1869) *Hereditary Genius*. (Second edition 1893.) London: Macmillan.

Gardner, H. (1983) *Frames of Mind: The Theory of Multiple Intelligences*. New York: Basic Books.

Gardner, M. K., Clark, E., (1992) 'The psychometric perspective on intellectual development in childhood and adolescence', in Sternberg, R. J., Berg, C. A. (eds) *Intellectual Development*, 16–44. Cambridge: Cambridge University Press.

Gardner, P. (1994) 'Diagnosing dyslexia in the classroom: a three-stage model', in Hales, G. (ed.) *Dyslexia Matters*. London: Whurr Publishers.

George, D. (1995) *Gifted Education: Identification and Provision*. London: David Fulton Publishers.

Glaister, G. (1976) The Service Family and Education of the Service Child. MA thesis, University of London.

Gleason, J. J. (1988) 'Spotting the camouflaged gifted student', *The Gifted Child Today* 11(3), 21–2.

Gottfried, A. W., Gottfied, A. E., Bathurst, K., Wright Guerin, D. (1994) *Gifted IQ. Early Developmental Aspects. The Fullerton Longitudinal Study*. New York: Plenum Press.

Gross, M. U. M. (1993) *Exceptionally Gifted Children*. London: Routledge.

Heatherington, E. M., Cox, M., Cox, R. (1978) 'The aftermath of divorce', in Stevens, J., Matthews, M. (eds) *Mother Child, Father Child Relations*. Washington, DC: National Association for the Education of Young Children.

Hegarty, S. (1993) *Meeting Special Needs in Ordinary Schools: An Overview*. London: Cassell.

Hegarty, S., Pocklington, K., Lucas, D. (1981) *Educating Pupils with Special Needs in Ordinary Schools*. Windsor: NFER-Nelson.

Hitchfield, E. M. (1973) *In Search of Promise: A Long Term National Study of Able Children and their Families*. London: Longman/ The National Children's Bureau.

HMI (1992) *The Education of Very Able Children in Maintained Schools*. London: HMSO.

Hymer, B., Harbron, N. (1998) 'Early transfer. A good move?', *Journal of NACE*, Spring, 38–47.

Kellmer Pringle, M. L. (1970) *Able Misfits: A Study of Educational and Behaviour Difficulties of 103 Very Intelligent Children*. London: Longman/ National Children's Bureau.

Kelly, G. A. (1955) *The Psychology of Personal Constructs*, Vols 1 & 2. New York: Norton.

Kent County Council (1995) *Able Children*. Canterbury: KCC.

Kulik, J., Kulik, C. (1984) 'Synthesis of research on effects of accelerated instruction', *Educational Leadership* 42(2), 84–9.

Lee-Corbin, H. (1984) A Study into the Effects of the Service Environment on the Academic Achievement of Army Children. Dissertation, University of Reading.

Lee-Corbin, H. (1996) Portraits of the Able Child: Factors Associated with Achievement and Under-Achievement. PhD thesis, University of Reading.

Maccoby, E., Jacklin, C. (1974) *Psychology of Sex Differences*. Stanford, CA: Stanford University Press.

Mboya, M. M. (1993) 'Self concept of academic abilities – relations with gender and academic achievement', *Perceptual and Motor Skills* 77(3), 1131–7.

McLanaghan, S. (1992) 'Intergenerational consequences of divorce: the United States perspective', in Weitzman, L. J., Maclean, M. (eds) *Economic Consequences of Divorce*. Oxford: Clarendon Press.

Miller, J. F. (1994) Disruptive Classroom Activities of Pupils who have Academic Potential. DPhil thesis, University of Oxford.

Mitchell, A. (1985) *Children in the Middle: Living Through Divorce*. London: Tavistock Publications.

Montgomery, D. (1996) *Educating the Able*. London: Cassell.

Mulkey, L. M., Crain, R. L., Harrington, A. J. C. (1992) 'One parent household and achievement', *Sociology of Education* 65, 48–65.

Nash, R. (1973) *Classrooms Observed*. London: Routledge and Kegan Paul.

National Association for Gifted Children (1990a) *Survey of provision for Gifted and Talented Children*. Northampton: NAGC.

National Association for Gifted Children (1990b) *According to Their Needs*. Northampton: NAGC.

National Association for Gifted Children (1995) 'Provision for the gifted in LEAs', *Looking to their Future: The Journal of the National Association for Gifted Children*, Winter, 1–3.

OFSTED (1995) 'Revision of the framework: national consultation', *OFSTED Update 13*.

Passow, A. (1958) 'Enrichment of education for the gifted', in Henry, M. (ed.) *Education for the Gifted: Fifty Seventh Yearbook of the National Society for the Study of Education, Part 1*, 193–221.

Patton, M. (1990) *Qualitative Evaluation and Research Methods*. Newbury Park, CA: Sage.

Plante, T. G., Goldfarb, L. P., Wadley, V. (1993) 'Are stress and coping associated with aptitude and achievement testing performance among children?', *Journal of School Psychology* 31(2), 259–66.

Pope, M., Denicolo, P. (1993) 'The art and science of constructivist research in teacher thinking', *Teaching and Teacher Education* 9(5/6), 529–44.

Pope, M., Keen, T. (1981) *Personal Construct Theory and Education*. London: Academic Press.

Quinn, V. (1997) *Critical Thinking in Young Minds*. London: David Fulton Publishers.

Raffan, J. (1996) 'Report on the NACE / DfE Project', *Looking to their Future: The Journal of the National Association for Gifted Children*, Spring.

Raven, J. C. (1991) *Standard Progressive Matrices*. Oxford: Psychologist's Press.

Renzulli, J. S. (1986) 'The three ring conception of giftedness: a developmental model for creative productivity', in Sternberg, R. J., Davidson J. H. (eds) *Conceptions of Giftedness*, 53–93, Cambridge: Cambridge University Press.

Renzulli, J. S. (1996) Effective Identification and Provision for Able and Exceptionally Able Pupils within Schools. Conference Presentation, Brunel University, November.

Robinson, M. (1991) *Family Transformation through Divorce and Remarriage*. London: Routledge.

Rosenthal, R., Jacobson, L. (1968) *Pygmalion in the Classroom*. New York: Holt, Rinehart and Winston.

Saracho, O. N. (1980) 'The relationship of teachers' cognitive style to pupils' academic achievement gains', *Journal of Educational Psychology* 77(4), 544–9.

Saracho, O. N. (1991) 'Teacher expectations and cognitive style: implications for students' academic achievement', *Early Child Development and Care* 77, 97–108.

Saracho, O. N. (1993) 'Sociocultural perspectives in the cognitive styles of young students and teachers', *Early Child Development and Care* 84, 1–17.

Smilansky, M., Nevo, D. (1979) *The Gifted Disadvantaged: A Ten Year Longitudinal Study of Compensatory Education in Israel*. London: Gordon and Breach.

Southern, W., Jones, E., Stanley, J. (1993) 'Acceleration and enrichment: the context and development of program options', in Heller, K., Monks, F., Passow, A. (eds) *International*

Handbook of Research and Development of Giftedness and Talent, 387–410. Oxford: Pergamon Press.

Stevenson, M., Black, K. (1995) *How Divorce Affects Offspring in a Research Approach*. Madison, Wis: Brown and Benchmark.

Tannenbaum, A. J. (1983) *Gifted Children: Psychological and Educational Perspectives*. New York: Macmillan.

Terman, L., Oden, M. (1926) *Genetic Studies of Genius*, Vol. 1. Stanford, CA: Stanford University Press.

Thomas, P. (1994) 'Writing, reading and gender', *Gifted Education International* **9**, 154–8.

Tiedemann, J., Faber, G. (1994) 'Girls and mathematics in elementary schools: results of a four year longitudinal study of gender differences in achievement', *Zeitscrift fur Entwicklung Psychologie und Padogogyische* **26**(2), 101–11.

Vantassel-Baska, J. (1993) 'Theory and research on curriculum development for the gifted', in Heller, K., Monks, F., Passow, A. (eds) *International Handbook of Research and Development of Giftedness and Talent*, 365–86. Oxford: Pergamon Press.

Warnock, M. (1988) *A Common Policy for Education*. Oxford: Oxford University Press.

Warrick, P. D., Naglieri, J. A. (1993) 'Gender differences in planning, attention, simultaneous and cognitive processes', *Journal of Educational Psychology* **85**(4), 693–701.

Weddell, K. (1980) 'Growing pains in understanding and assessing perceptuo-motor problems', in McKinlay, G. N. (ed.) *Helping Clumsy Children*, 40–52. London: Longman.

Weisner, T. S., Garnier, H. (1992) 'Non-conventional family life-styles and school achievement', *American Educational Research Journal* **29**(3), 605–32.

Whitmore, J. (1980) *Giftedness, Conflict and Underachievement*. Boston: Allyn and Bacon.

Whitmore, J. (1986) 'Recognising and developing hidden giftedness', *The Elementary School Journal* **82**(3), 275–83.

Whitmore, J. (1988) 'Gifted children at risk for learning difficulties', *Teaching Exceptional Children* **20**(4), 10–14.

Williams, E. (1995) 'Lapped by girls', *Times Educational Supplement* **14**(7), 3–5.

Winter S. (1993) 'What do Hong Kong teachers expect of high performing and low performing pupils?' *Psychologia* **36**(3), 167–78.

Witkin, H. A. (1962) *Psychological Differentiation: Studies of Development*. Chichester: Wiley.

Witkin, H. A., Goodenough, D. (1977) 'Field dependence and interpersonal behaviour'. *Psychological Bulletin* **84**(4), 661–89.

Witkin, H. A., Oltman, P. K., Raskin, E., Karp, S. A. (1971) *Group Embedded Figures Test*. California: Consulting Psychologists Press.

Witty, P. (1951) *The Gifted Child*. Boston: Heath.

Wood (1983) 'Poem for Everyman', in *How Do You Feel?* London: Prentice Hall.

Index

Printed in the United Kingdom
by Lightning Source UK Ltd.
130456UK00009B/56/A